PORTFOLIO
100 TIPS TO CRACK THE IIT

VIVEK PANDEY has a BTech in computer science and an MTech in industrial management, both from the Indian Institute of Technology, Kanpur, and an MBA from the Indian School of Business. He has held leadership positions in marketing and product development in the Internet industry and is currently building a new product. He lives in Delhi with his wife, Ruchi, and their children, Sipul and Rohin.

PARAS ARORA is an entrepreneur, a friend, a critic and a consultant, not necessarily in that order. He has a BTech from the Indian Institute of Technology, Guwahati, and an MBA from the Indian School of Business, Hyderabad. He loves taking chances, making friends, connecting people and learning continuously.

100 Tips
to Crack the
IIT

VIVEK PANDEY
&
PARAS ARORA

PORTFOLIO
PENGUIN

An imprint of Penguin Random House

PORTFOLIO

USA | Canada | UK | Ireland | Australia
New Zealand | India | South Africa | China | Singapore

Portfolio is part of the Penguin Random House group of
companies whose addresses can be found at global.penguinrandomhouse.com

Published by Penguin Random House India Pvt. Ltd
4th Floor, Capital Tower 1, MG Road,
Gurugram 122 002, Haryana, India

Penguin
Random House
India

First published in Portfolio by Penguin Books India 2013

ISBN 9780143419761

Typeset in Dante Mt Std by Eleven Arts, New Delhi
Printed at Repro India Limited

www.penguin.co.in

MIX
Paper from
responsible sources
FSC® C047271

To my mother who brought me into this world and the alma maters that made me worth it.

—Vivek Pandey

*

To my niece Soumya, who gives us a reason to smile every single day.

—Paras Arora

CONTENTS

CONTENTS

CONTENTS

CONTENTS

CONTENTS

Acknowledgements

This work would not have been possible without Ruchi forcing me to believe in myself and without Sipul and Rohin not partially sacrificing their inalienable right on my time.

                                                              Vivek Pandey

                                   *

This book would not have been possible without the support of my family. All that I have learnt from life has been because of my mother, Shashi Arora. I was blessed to have her as my first teacher and guide. She is the one who opened my mind to learning and this book draws upon the ideas and methods she used to teach me when I was a kid. A special thanks to my dad, Dr Harish Arora, for making learning exciting for me by setting up new challenges on the way and showering me with gifts when I triumphed. I would like to thank Dr Parul Arora and Dr Nishant Arora for inspiring me to achieve greater heights and supporting me in all my endeavours.

ACKNOWLEDGEMENTS

I am particularly indebted to my friends Ankit Nagori, Brij Mohan Vashisth, Divya Devesh, Saurabh Nangia, Shravni Jain for reviewing my work and providing invaluable inputs and feedback while I was writing this book.

Paras Arora

Authors' Note

We want this book to be your companion and guide while you prepare for the JEE and not an overbearing, boring tome that will waste your time. The narrative is as conversational, friendly and intimate as possible, sharing with you many of our personal experiences and learning secrets. We decided to keep the narrative voice singular (that is, 'I', 'me', 'mine'), instead of plural ('we', 'us', 'our'), so that you relate one-on-one to what we're saying rather than feel oppressed by having two people telling you what to do. Where an experience is particular to one of us, we've indicated whose it is at the bottom of the page.

What Is the IIT?

'The IITs have become an integral constituent of what is known as Brand India,' said Prime Minister Dr Manmohan Singh at the golden jubilee convocation of the Indian Institute of Technology (IIT), Bombay. This unstinting belief that the IITs are the breeding ground of excellence has been passed down for generations since they were founded in the 1950s and '60s. The IITs have been the ultimate dream of the Indian middle class, a key to unlock their fortunes. When the Big B quips *gyan hi aapko aapka haq dilata hai* (knowledge alone gets you what you rightfully deserve), it reiterates the belief based on which these institutes were conceived by Pandit Jawaharlal Nehru.

The intention was actually much grander: the IITs were supposed to be one of the pillars of the Mahalanobis approach to build a modern India on education and industry. But to the common man, IIT is the quintessential mantra of success. Brand IIT has withstood the changing contours of the Indian economy. While it was once defined by the IITians who dotted the Silicon Valley, it is now being remoulded by the IITians who dominate the entrepreneurial and corporate corridors in India.

The IIT-JEE (Joint Entrance Examination) is the common entrance test for all the IITs. More than 5 lakh candidates appeared for the JEE in 2012. Only about 10,000 got selected, making the pass percentage a meagre 2 per cent. This also means every student who gets selected is better than at least 4,90,000 other students. Notwithstanding how easy or tough the exam is, the sheer numbers make clearing the bar in JEE an uphill task. The pattern of the JEE keeps changing; and the number and length of the papers, the nature of the questions, etc., change almost every year. What does not change is the uncanny ability of the JEE to rank lakhs of students by their suitability to be the top engineers and scientists of the world.

WHY IIT? WHY JEE?

Exactly when does it start in one's head, this idea of getting into IIT? Ask yourself. When did you first hear the word IIT? Class eleven? Nine? Six? Nursery? In your mother's womb? I first heard of IIT from my best friend when I was in class nine.* (My best friend of class nine, because, as it goes, in school best friends change every year.) Very soon

* This relates to Vivek. Henceforth indicated by 'Vivek'.

the three-letter acronym became this magical pathway to victory. From the first moment onward, it became a challenge for me, a never-never land of promises meant only for the chosen few, the proverbial end of the rainbow where the pot of gold lies. I believe it was no different from an *Indian Idol* or a *Dance India Dance* to me at that time—a badge that got you recognition in the vast Indian Ocean of anonymity teeming with countless nameless faces and faceless names. It was a panacea for all ills, a once-in-a-lifetime opportunity to set everything right in my life.

My parents saw it as a way for me to secure my career, assure myself a livelihood and eventually 'settle down'. What students of your age need most is inspiration to do something really big and make their lives special. In some ways this is actually rather biological as I am sure even the neurological and hormonal systems know that this is the best time to set oneself up for something BIG in life. IIT is just that—the opportunity to do something really, really BIG.

So IIT gives you the best start and provides you a platform to launch yourself and unlock your potential. But when it comes to building or securing your future, even with mathematics as your subject of choice in school, the IITs are not the only way to secure it. Never think of IIT as the *only* pathway to success. Such a point of view will never be able to motivate you and will only create undue pressure. If your IIT-JEE does not go according to plan and you don't make it, please realize that there are many more options to make a successful (and peaceful) life and career.

Ask yourself what kind of person you really are. What do you want most? Do you want to get really (really!) rich? Or do you want to get comfortable? Do you want to be popular? Do you want to do something for your country? And be honest; don't fool yourself. There is nothing wrong in wanting any of these. Honesty is most important. You should be looking to get into an IIT if you have:

FIT FOR IIT

- Belief in the power of science and technology to change lives
- A deep interest in and understanding of core scientific principles
- Ability to take responsibility for one's life and maintain discipline
- A desire to disagree meaningfully and explore something new

This actually aligns well with the 'Primary Objectives' of the IITs as stated in the 2013 JEE brochure (which you must read, if you haven't already; it can be very inspiring).

These objectives are:
- Build a solid foundation of scientific and technical

knowledge and thus to prepare competent and motivated engineers and scientists

- Create an environment for freedom of thought, cultivate vision, encourage growth, develop personality and self-discipline for the pursuit of excellence
- Kindle an entrepreneurial streak in the students

However, the above three qualities are not essential for you to clear JEE. Studying at IIT and clearing the JEE are two *very* separate things. To clear the JEE you just need to:

FIT FOR JEE

- Understand what the examiner is looking to test in you
- Work hard enough to perfect the JEE syllabus
- Be great at time management while taking the exam

As you can see, the two are very different sets of requirements.

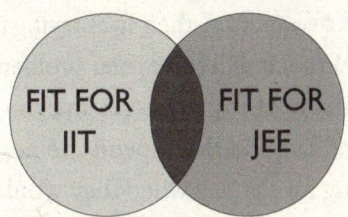

There are people who are a great fit for the IIT, but cannot get through JEE because they don't have the ability or the knack to clear the exam. Almost all IITians have had people like these in their schools or coaching classes. They loved science, were extremely responsible and disciplined, but somehow weren't able to crack the JEE. Every time you think of them you feel that they *should* have been in IIT, that they *deserved* to be in an IIT, but they could never make it.

Then there are others who are great at cracking the JEE but don't have the scientific spirit or the discipline to fit into the IITs. These are the students who lose interest in IIT the moment they land there. These are the ones who try to create alternative lives for themselves outside of classrooms and examinations. Of course, all of them are smart (they cleared the JEE, didn't they!), so they end up doing something great with their lives anyway. But the IIT infrastructure is of no use to them. All the books, professors, labs and lectures are lost on them. Probably they could have done even better in a different college which suited their interests more.

My fear with these others is that they (and their families) invest a precious two years of their lives trying to crack the JEE in the fond belief that it will solve their problems once and for all. I have seen many of my peers get stuck in the IIT system due to this mentality and then spend the next four years of their lives waiting for the day when they would be 'free' from IIT and be able to start a life of their own. Lots of them give up on the place within days of entering it. By the second year so many students are already preparing for the next big thing, which could be either CAT (Common Admission Test) or IAS (Indian Administrative Service) or anything else that will take them away from engineering. The net result is, six years of your life invested in a disastrous trip just to get the IIT badge. Don't get me wrong. I have that badge and it is an honour to have it, and it does help you a lot in life. But is it the best you can do for yourself? More importantly, is it the only way to get ahead in life? It is sad how restricted our imagination can be when it comes to our own lives.

The real gems are those in the intersection between these two groups. These are the students who are a fine mix of being responsible, disciplined and smart, besides having a scientific spirit. They derive the maximum benefit from the IIT system and end up in places where they want and love to be. It is usually alumni like them who have made brand IIT what it is today.

All said and done, what is most important is that you have to know clearly whether you and IIT are compatible, whether you and JEE are compatible and how you would use the IIT degree to be useful to the world and successful in life.

The Tips

Having briefed and warned you in great detail, it is time now to dive into the tips that I have curated for you. I have exactly 100 tips, which are divided into the following sections. I strongly believe that if you are able to diligently understand and assimilate these tips into your life, your goal of getting into an IIT will come much, much closer. *All the best!*

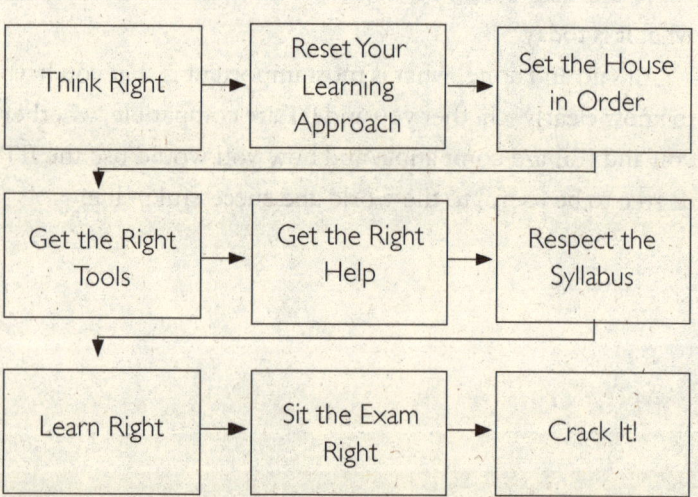

THINK RIGHT

1. Know What You *Don't* Want

> 'Missing a train is only painful if you run after it! Likewise,
> not matching the idea of success others expect from you
> is only painful if that's what you are seeking.'
> —Nassim Nicholas Taleb

Over the years, everybody around me—parents, friends, colleagues, teachers, random people on flights, trains and buses—has asked me what I want to do with my life.[*] I have always found it the most perplexing question, a question I don't even know how to start answering. My answers ranged from going on a trek to the Himalayas, becoming a poet, opening an art cafe, starting an Internet business to studying engineering. Clearly, I had no concrete view of what I wanted to do. So, I deflected the question and instead asked people what they thought I should do with my life. And along came the most clichéd replies—become a doctor or an engineer or a chartered accountant, etc.

Unsatisfied, I thought hard about the question. I questioned the question itself. I was unsure whether a right answer could ever exist for this kind of question. Then I thought about answering a simpler but related question: What is it that I *don't* want to do with my life? Now, this

---

[*] This relates to Paras. Henceforth indicated by 'Paras'.

was something that I could answer with some certainty. I was certain that I did not want to become a doctor (the thickness of books and over nine years of study was enough to turn me off). I was certain I could not become an artist (for if I couldn't explore a single creative talent in eighteen years, there was nothing much to look forward to on that front). Looking back, I think figuring out what I didn't want, rather than trying to think of what I really wanted, helped me stay clear of random career suggestions that other people made.

'Turtle' the question. Whenever you find yourself in a position where you don't know what to do or which path to take, try and answer a simpler question: Which path should you not take? I think it will help you clear away a lot of clutter from your head and make you more focused. No matter what people say, you alone are capable of understanding your abilities and your likings. Remember, it's easy to give in to what your friends are doing, it's easy to run with the crowd but you are not the crowd, you are unique and you have to make a choice that suits you well.

Why the choice matters. Over the past few years, I have seen many students preparing for IIT drop out after class eleven. They are just not able to cope with the pressure that comes with preparing for a competitive exam, while pursuing regular studies. More often than not, the reason for backing out midway is because it wasn't their choice to go for IIT in the first place. Sometimes their parents made this choice for them and at other times they just followed what their friends were doing. So, if I were you, I would avoid such a disaster as it will not get me anywhere. Before you go ahead with this book, take out some time and reflect on what you like and dislike, what kind of career you want. Go talk to your teachers, seniors, parents and relatives. Figure out what they did with their lives and ask them how they could have made better choices. Help is all around, you just have to seek it.

To help you with this, I have tried to prepare a brief summary of various career choices that you can make and what you can expect out of those choices. Please remember that these are personal assessments and are for indicative purposes only. All the rating is on a scale of 5, where 1 is very low and 5 is very high.

	Engineering	Medical	BBA/MBA	CA	Law
Work–Life Balance	3	3	3	4	4
Peer Group	5	5	5	5	5
Growth	3	5	3	4	4
Financial Stability	4	4	4	4	4

2. Are You Intelligent?

How many times have you heard the words 'He is so intelligent'? I don't think you can count them. And, most of the time, it is applied to certain kinds of individuals who can solve problems quickly or score well in exams. Do we even know what 'being intelligent' means? Let me quote a definition of intelligence which a group of fifty-two researchers agreed upon in 1994:

> A very general mental capability that, among other things, involves the ability to reason, plan, solve problems, think abstractly, comprehend complex ideas, learn quickly and learn from experience. *It is not merely book learning, a narrow academic skill, or test-taking ability.* Rather, it reflects a broader and deeper capability for comprehending our surroundings— 'catching on', 'making sense' of things, or 'figuring out' what to do [emphasis mine].*

So, calling someone intelligent just because they have programmed themselves to solve certain kinds of problems faster or are able to score well in tests, is a little narrow-minded. Intelligence is a much larger concept; it is the sum total of the responses people give to all kinds of life situations. Trust me, a JEE rank, or even the fact that someone got through JEE, is only a limited measure of how 'intelligent' he or she is. The moment you start thinking like that, you condition yourself to believe that some people are inherently predisposed towards succeeding in JEE while the 'not-so-intelligent' fellows are doomed to fail. It is a big *lie* that your parents, your teachers

---

* 'Mainstream Science on Intelligence', statement published in the *Wall Street Journal*, 13 December 1994. See Linda S. Gottfredson, 'Mainstream Science on Intelligence (editorial)', *Intelligence* 24: 13–23, http://www.udel.edu/educ/gottfredson/reprints/1997mainstream.pdf.

and your peers have been telling you; most of the time, it is an excuse for some failure on their own part. Just because they did not have the intelligence to explain something in a better way, they labelled you as not intelligent enough to understand. I have seen classes being taken by hopeless teachers and terrible books that pass judgement on students' intelligence or lack thereof. I think it is misplaced arrogance. They should be worrying more about their own ability to teach, write and communicate the concepts to the students rather than commenting upon the intelligence of people. The next time someone calls you 'not intelligent', feel insulted and fight back. Don't accept this judgement.

Intelligence is also very different from and only weakly correlated with academic ability. Academic ability is absorbing what is offered to you and then using that to solve problems in that specific academic context. But acts based on intelligence happen throughout a person's life, at times without them even knowing it. Reading a map and remembering its finer details while finding your way around is ability; knowing that a particular route is going to be useless today because it is the rainy season is intelligence. Doing the toughest of assignments by applying your theory and mind is ability; being able to avoid the teacher's wrath without doing the homework is intelligence.

What does JEE have to do with intelligence anyway? Cracking JEE is not about intelligence at all. No research study that exists has been able to prove that JEE ranks, or ranks or scores in any exam, are significantly correlated to a person's intelligence quotient, or IQ. Success in JEE is all about programming yourself to succeed in the examination; and there are just two things that are important:

- Knowing what programming has to be done; call it the 'formula to succeed', if you will
- A passion for doing that programming, to the finest details

The more you know about the programming and the more passionate you are about perfecting it, the better your chance of succeeding. All of us who are average or somewhat average have the exact same chance of succeeding in the JEE, and in fact in anything in life.

3. Be the Effort in the Effortless

Riding my bike on a cold morning from Noida to South Delhi, on my way to collecting the snack supplies for my cafe, I thought about the contrast in the perspectives of the customers who eat at a cafe and the staff who actually run it.* For people who order a sandwich, it all seems easy. The server takes out the sandwich from the display counter, grills it, puts it on a plate, places some ketchup and tissue paper next to it and hands it over. Easy. Not much hard work involved; seemingly effortless. However, those who run the show have to make sure they drive to the bakery early morning, pick up the fresh

* Paras.

supplies, check whether the grill is working and that there are enough paper plates and ketchup sachets, and so on. For them it is a lot of hard work; in short, a lot of effort goes into making sure a customer can enjoy a sandwich without hassle. It was on this bike ride that I realized that there is so much effort that goes into making anything effortless. This principle has stayed with me since then and I believe it is applicable to all walks of life, including JEE preparations.

You would have often heard people say that mathematics comes naturally to some people, that some people just have a flair for numbers. But that's only one half of the story. While there is no doubt that some people are gifted and have special skills, what the onlookers miss is the effort that goes into honing a skill and making it work to one's advantage. The people who find maths effortless have actually put in a lot of hard work and effort at some point of time, perhaps when they were in middle school or high school. Knowledge greatly depends on strong fundamentals. So, the earlier in life you start strengthening your fundamentals, the less effort you will have to put in later. Talent does what it can, but after that it's up to you to harvest it and convert it into genius. No matter how smart you are, no matter how sharp you are, nothing worthwhile comes without a fight and the same logic applies to cracking the JEE.

People who've made it through the JEE will tell you that it was not that tough and that they got through without much effort. They say it because they worked hard, put in a lot of effort and eventually found cracking the exam effortless. No matter what people say, the next two years of your life will require you to put in a lot of effort. You will have to stick to a routine and study hard. You will have to be judicious with your time and not while it away on random things. This does not meant that you'll have to become a bookworm. You'll just have to manage your time so that you can still squeeze in a movie over the weekend and hang out with your friends.

Before you move on to the next section of the book, get ready to face challenges, getting stuck with problems, feeling a little lost sometimes or feeling like giving up. Just remember that you are tougher than any problem. Just keep putting in your best and you shall tame the beast that is the JEE.

4. Mental Conditioning

Have you seen a dog on the street that has its tail between its legs all the time, who gets startled at the slightest movement around it and runs for dear life the moment you bend down as if to pick up a stone? And have you seen the dog that is inside the gates of a grand mansion, who growls and barks at everyone who passes by and makes life hell for his master if it's not taken out for its regular evening stroll? They are both dogs, but they have been trained differently by their circumstances and experiences. It is the manifestation of a popular Mark Twain saying, that 'it is not the size of the dog in the fight but the size of the fight in the dog'.

Think of your mind as a dog that you have to train. If you

keep thinking about failure, about what will happen if you don't get selected, about that other student in class who is so 'intelligent' and will surely top the JEE, then your mind is getting conditioned for failure. You are training it to expect and accept failure. If, however, you keep dreaming about the day when you will get a rank in the top 100 in JEE, keep feeling awesome about your unique methods of learning and believe there are very few who can really compete with you, then *you are conditioning your mind for success*. Life and success are largely games of self-belief. If you believe in yourself, you will keep on trying and will not be bogged down by roadblocks that you may hit from time to time. At the same time you must understand that there's a fine line between self-belief and complacency. Complacency is dangerous, and negativity is far more dangerous. So, condition yourself all the time for a successful outcome of your preparation.

There is this very interesting case of five monkeys who were locked together in a cage with a banana plant inside. One monkey at a time was allowed to get atop the tree to eat a banana. Every time a monkey ate a banana, the other monkeys had cold water thrown over them. After a couple of such instances, every time a monkey tried to reach for the bananas, the other monkeys would start screaming.

The monkey going for the banana would get scared and give up its attempt. One by one the monkeys in the cage were replaced with new ones from outside. So, at any given point, there would always be a few monkeys in the group that had joined later and had never had water thrown over them. But they too joined in the screaming when any monkey went for the bananas. Gradually, all the monkeys in the cage were replaced so that now there was no monkey in the cage that had ever had cold water thrown over it. Still, none of the new monkeys went for the bananas as they were all scared of the screaming and social ostracizing that came with it.

The case of the five monkeys will tell you how easily one can fall into the trap of 'this cannot be done' or 'should not be done' just because the people around you who are saying so have failed in the past. We are human beings, not monkeys. No matter what anyone says, you have to attempt what you believe in.

5. Know Thyself

All roads lead to Rome but the roads are all different. So, know thy road and know thyself. The human mind is a complex piece of machinery and every single one of us thrives in unique circumstances. You should think about how, when and where you think well. Mornings never worked for me for rigorous study and, somehow, sitting in a crowded place made me concentrate more.[*] Placing my hands over my ears helped me concentrate better. You have to know these things about your own mind. Also figure out whether you thrive in a group-study scenario or prefer to go solo. If you do well in a group, make

[*] Vivek.

sure the group has diversity in terms of subject strength and has a good balance of seriousness and fun.

Find ways to train and exercise your mind. Fifteen minutes of Sudoku, half an hour of sketching or maybe even your favourite Playstation game. All these help jog the mind and keep it fresh. Find ways to chill out mentally. Music works for most people. Maybe walking around or talking to a neighbour works for you. Five minutes spent with an inspiring great-uncle can give your mind wings and five minutes with a pesky aunt can leave it gasping for air. Watch out for demotivating and disparaging people.

Specific to studies, find your pets and peeves among the subjects. Pets drain time, peeves drain energy. Getting upset while deriving an equation might sound bad, but knowing beforehand that it might upset you is quite good. And maybe reading that treasury of short stories makes you feel awesome, but somewhere you have to stop and check the watch. Remember, before you can learn a subject you have to like it. So if you don't like a subject condition yourself to like it before you start studying it.

Most of all, figure out how you learn best. Some people are visual learners, that is, they learn better through pictures or sketches; some prefer auditory methods, and they learn better by talking to or listening to someone; and some are kinaesthetic and learn better by playing things out. There are standard tests available (search for VAK tests) that help you identify what works for you and devise methods of learning accordingly.

6. You Are Your Biggest Competition

In order to make it through JEE, you need to forget about the competition. Yes, this sounds odd but let's explore this a little further. There are two reasons why I say that to achieve your best, you have to forget about competing against others.

Competing against others limits our ability to achieve our full potential. When we compete against others, we push ourselves only hard enough to beat them. The benchmark in this case is set by our competitors. The competition defines the level we need to attain to come out on top, which is generally lower than our true potential. It is human to try only as hard as is sufficient. Very few people are able to push themselves to their limits. It's a classic case of being internally driven versus being driven by the competition. So, in order to achieve your best, you have to become your own competition.

Beating your competition a few times breeds complacency. You cannot do more harm to yourself than by becoming complacent. Complacency gives you nothing but a false sense of security and superiority. The moment you step out of your comfort zone of known competitors, reality will hit you hard in the face. The reason coaching classes are so successful is not because they teach anything unique; it is because there you compete against the best in the country and this competition keeps you on your toes. Remember, you have to raise the bar even higher if you are already the best in your circle. History is littered with people who fell from the top because they thought they were invincible. Their false sense of superiority was what got them finally. And then there are the few who went on to become the greatest not because they were competing against anyone else (in most cases they were far ahead of their competitors) but because they knew they could do better each time. Remember, Sachin Tendulkar is the best out there, but he still never misses a net practice session. The race is long and in the end it is only against yourself.

You are as smart as the people around you. Accept that you may not be the best in everything. Each one of us has certain strengths and certain weaknesses. Recognizing your weaknesses and working on them is perhaps the best possible thing that you can do for yourself. Now you must be wondering where the competition fits in in all of this. Well, when we blindly compete with others, we lose a chance to learn from their strengths and work on our weaknesses. There is no collaboration in an environment of cut-throat competition.

As the adage goes, 'To create a successful business, hire people who are smarter than you.' Similarly, to improve yourself, find people who are better than you and learn from them. Forget about competition and create an atmosphere of collaboration. Learn from others' strengths and work on your weaknesses. This approach will not only help you improve yourself but also make you more humble about your weaknesses. In the end, you will not only become a better version of yourself, but also make some lifelong friends.

7. Lonely at the Top

You will clear the JEE with an awesome rank if *you* want it, not because your mother or best friend or the world wants it. And if you are not willing to make sacrifices it will not happen. If you want to live a balanced life, have fun with friends, watch movies, not miss your favourite TV shows, play soccer and live a life of variety, you are setting yourself up for a great life ahead. *Yet, you will not clear the JEE unless you put in a little extra effort towards your studies and let go of time-wasting activities.* The balance has to be tilted in favour of studies if you want to realize your dream. You have to believe that once you earn that rank, you can compensate for these sacrifices when you are in IIT. It is called delayed gratification and it is the key to committing yourself to the goal of being at the top.

And, finally, about that secret page that successful JEE aspirants read before the exam: it is a page full of inspiration. It is a page that will help you find your way and keep you motivated during the tough times. Each one of us draws inspiration and motivation from different sources, and as such this final page is highly customized to suit one's individual needs. Some have quotes, some have pictures, some have their mother's letters and some have couplets from their favourite poems or from the Ramayana or the Quran. Inspiration in some form or the other is required. As they say, success is 99 per cent perspiration and 1 per cent inspiration, and the last 1 per cent plays a very important role in cracking the JEE.

RESET YOUR LEARNING APPROACH

8. Let Your Mind Wander

Confucius was absolutely right when he said, 'I hear I forget, I see I remember, I do I learn.' *There is no substitute for learning by doing.* When you experience something in its physical form, get to touch and feel it, the experience gets imprinted on to your long-term memory. Whenever you think of something connected to this experience, you will easily recall the vivid details associated with it. You will relive the experience over and over again. Your mind will take you back in time and you will be able to see yourself performing the task. For example, when someone describes the Himalayas to you, you can immediately visualize a snow-clad mountain that you may have seen and can actually feel the chill by relating it to how cold you felt when you were near a snow-clad mountains or hill station. This ability of the mind to help you relive an experience can be of great help while preparing for JEE. The JEE syllabus covers a lot of practical concepts such as electric currents, motors, motion, rotation, chemical reactions, etc., which find their application in various day-to-day things you see and do. You must make sure that you get your hands dirty and give yourself an experience to relate to what you are reading in the classroom. The reason I still remember the parts of a motor and the logic behind its working is that I actually opened a small motor and saw what was inside it.*

* Paras.

If you chase learning, the marks will follow. It will help you not just pass a particular class or standard but help you grasp things better as you progress through your academic and professional career. Nowadays, especially with kids handling an average of eight subjects a year, it becomes all the more important to explore the practical side of classroom learning.

So, what exactly do I mean by learning by doing? Here's an example: Despite being an engineer and having last studied biology in class ten, I still remember the parts of a flower—petals, stamen, pollen—not because I have a sharp memory but because my mother plucked a flower from our garden, dissected it and showed the different parts to me.[*] That's it. This is all that you need to transfer something into your long-term memory. Whenever I pick a flower and look at its parts, my mind takes me back in time to where I can see my mother showing me the different parts and helping me understand their purposes. So just keep on asking, how can I experience this, or where can I see the application of what I learnt today in class?

Now, you may think that it is easy for you to experience various concepts in physics and chemistry as almost all things around us are governed by some law of either physics or chemistry or both. But you may feel that mathematics is more about conceptual learning and it is difficult to visualize mathematical concepts. I beg to differ and would like to use an

[*] Paras.

24

example to demonstrate how you can visualize mathematical concepts. Let's try the basic $(a + b)^2 = a^2 + b^2 + 2ab$.

Draw a line of length $a + b$. As we are interested in finding $(a + b)$ squared, let's complete a square around that line, such that the length of the square is $a + b$.

Now join the opposite sides at lengths 'a' respectively. Calculate the area of each of the smaller quadrilaterals.

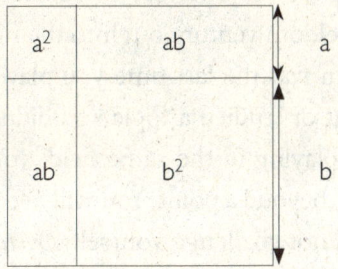

Adding up the areas of all four quadrilaterals (two squares and two rectangles) we get $a^2 + b^2 + ab + ab = a^2 + b^2 + 2ab$.

So, go out there, buy that experiment kit, pluck a few flowers, break and fix (hopefully) a few things, help your father with the tools, help your mother with the cooking. Just keep your eyes open, ears alert and hands busy. You will be surprised at the ways in which your classroom concepts will materialize in the most unexpected of places.

9. Don't Overwork Your Strengths

Everybody loves to succeed. We like it when we are able to win and come out on top. Our love for success and loathing for failure finds expression in our workplaces, in playgrounds, in studies and almost everywhere else. Yearning for success is great but the fear of failure is bad. It is better to fail than to fear failure. There is no better teacher than failure; it builds a person's character and gives them the perseverance they need to reach their goal.

Given our love for success, we develop a tendency to avoid situations where we are not very comfortable. We like to play it safe and seldom venture out into the unknown or the unfamiliar. When was the last time you played a game you were not good at or studied a topic you didn't really enjoy? If you keep on playing in the same field, you will not add value to yourself beyond a point. You will become a little too comfortable and not challenge yourself. *Overdoing something that you are good at is generally not a good thing, especially when it comes to IIT-JEE, where you need to score in all three subjects.*

Ace one and miss cut-offs on others: I have seen my classmates and younger cousin focus too much on mathematics or physics because they loved the subject and were good at it.[*] They would buy all the books in the market and solve almost every problem. However, they failed to realize that the additional utility of solving yet another mathematics problem was much less than focusing on a different subject, say, chemistry or physics. Yes, they did have a scoring subject (one they did really well in) but in reality, they were only as strong as their weakest

[*] Paras.

subject. The rule of JEE is that you have to clear the minimum cut-off in all three subjects; this makes it essential for you to give comparable if not equal attention to physics, chemistry *and* maths. You just cannot ignore one subject and keep on practising only those subjects that you love and are good at.

Focus on all three subjects. You may not like a few topics, but JEE is not designed according to what you like or dislike. Albert Einstein once said, 'Know the rules of the game and then play it better than everybody else,' and the JEE rule of the game is that organic chemistry counts as much as trigonometry. So, make it a point to devote at least two hours a day to the subject that you like the least. The more effort you put into it, the easier it will get to bear it if not love it. It is generally better to start your day with your weakest subject. This means that you start reading your weakest (and least favourite) subject with a fresh mind and can look forward to finishing it so that you can get back to your favourite subjects. If you don't want to start your day like this, then keep the least favourite as a filler subject. Break it down into four sessions of half an hour each. This way you will not get bored and may actually enjoy small doses of that subject.

10. It's All about Balance

Yes, JEE requires a lot of hard work and dedication, but one has to be smart about how to approach it. You only have twenty-four hours in a day and you have to use them efficiently. One of the most common mistakes aspirants make is to indiscriminately solve as many problems as they can. I have often seen students prepare a topic from ten different books. They pick up every book available and just keep solving problems. Practising is great, but JEE is not about merely solving problems. It is a test of your concepts and there is no direct correlation between the number of questions you solve and how conceptually strong you are on a topic. So don't panic if your friends are solving problems from every possible book out there. Don't bother picking up substandard books (they will often have wrong solutions). *Just focus on understanding the basics and stick to a few recommended books from the best authors there are.* Give time to each and every question, especially those which you could not solve in a couple of tries. When you attempt a problem, don't start solving it right away; build an approach in your head, figure out the underlying principles involved and think how you can apply the concepts and tools that you have learnt in class to that particular problem. Don't just apply the formulae. It will make your thinking shallow and will deprive you of real learning.

Another issue with just blindly solving problems is that you will keep making the same mistakes over and over again. If we focus on merely doing as many problems as possible, we do not give ourselves the time to reflect on our mistakes and revisit the concepts. We just think that the next time we won't make the same mistake, but we are bound to falter again because the underlying concept is flawed, and there are only so many mistakes that one can remember. So, focus on the concepts. If you make a mistake, take some time and reflect on the concept and figure out where you went wrong. Don't focus on the number of problems; instead, focus on the problem in problems.

How many problems are enough? Now you must be wondering how many problems you should solve for a particular concept—10, 20, 50, 100 or 500? My answer is that it's not really about the number of problems but the *type* of problems you solve. There has to be a gradual increase in the difficulty level of problems as you move ahead with a concept. The problems have to involve multiple concepts (sometimes across different topics). You can solve a thousand problems of the same type and yet be stumped when the JEE exam asks you a slightly twisted problem from the same concept. Therefore, place greater focus on solving different types of problems. Ask your friends about the interesting or difficult problems they have encountered in a topic. Bounce problems off them and see their approach, understand their thought processes and compare them with yours. See where you can learn from them and where you can contribute.

11. Learn to Learn

There are so many new things to learn when preparing for JEE. Some people learn fast, others, slowly. The former are made to believe that they are smarter than the rest and hence they learn faster. This is wrong. While there are certainly some differences between the mental faculties of people (as reflected partially in their IQ scores and partially in their EQ), these differences can be bridged and are not permanent. Learning itself is an art that you have to learn. Learning does not mean just memorizing. For me, it involves developing perspectives.* Can you look up at the sun today with a new perspective? That it is a fusion reactor. Can you look at yourself with a different perspective? That you have evolved from a chimpanzee. *It is about challenging your intuition, opening up your mind to new possibilities and developing new perspectives about things that you already knew but saw differently.*

How you can do that is the bigger question though. It comes through a little bit of humility and trust. You should be humble enough to accept that there is a lot out there that you don't know and should know. And you should trust that whatever is being taught to you through books and question banks is for your own good.

12. Free Your Conscious Mind

Friedrich Schelling from Germany introduced the term 'unconscious mind'. The unconscious mind is the part of our thinking that runs on autopilot. Consider the time when you cycle home. Do you actually think about cycling during that time? Avoiding obstacles, taking turns, even finding the way from school to home happens automatically. You don't

* Vivek.

have to spare a thought to it. Your thoughts are of course wandering around more interesting things! The routine, boring activities that you perform repetitively are all slowly moved to the unconscious mind, leaving the conscious mind to focus on the most important and most interesting parts of your day.

When something becomes part of your unconscious mind, it becomes part of your system and doesn't require much effort to reproduce as and when required. So, whenever you are learning new things, the endeavour should be to learn them so well that they move, as much as possible, to your unconscious mind. The unconscious mind has almost an infinite capacity, while the conscious mind has a very limited capacity. This is what super rote-learners do when they are trying to memorize something—keep repeating it again and again so that it moves to the unconscious. But the problem is that the unconscious mind is not a board into which you can hammer nails by force. It makes decisions of its own when storing things. It retains something if it finds it either very important or very interesting. If you try to learn things that your unconscious mind determines as neither important to your survival nor interesting enough, it will reject them.

So make sure, whenever you are trying to learn something, that you understand and accept the importance of learning it (not the necessity but the importance) and you either find it interesting or make it interesting. Only then will it become part of your unconscious mind.

13. Visualize the Problems

Creating visualizations of problems is a great way to improve your focus and break down a complex problem into simpler, manageable parts. Especially in physics, it is very important to make visual representations of problem situations. These visual representations could be mental or physical drawings, depending on what you can do faster and better. (It's always better to create physical drawings as it lets your mind break the problem down and attack it in small parts.) Don't worry too much about actual measurements but the visual should be roughly to scale. When you are early into your preparation, or beginning a new topic, try and physically draw the problem in each and every case. Try and put yourself through the drawing, how the pulley would have moved, how the current would have circulated in the circuit, what would have been the trajectory of the ball, etc. As you practise, you will realize you don't need to actually draw things for simpler problems as the image immediately becomes clear in your head. But whenever a problem is even slightly complex, it helps to draw things. Some of you might believe initially that this is an overhead. I think it is an investment. Gradually, you will get quicker and quicker at doing it and you will begin to see the rewards.

Let's take an example: Problem No. 7, JEE Physics 1998

A solid body X of heat capacity C is kept in an atmosphere whose temperature is $T_A = 300K$. At time t = 0, the temperature of X is T_0 = 400K. It cools according to Newton's Law of Cooling. At time t_1 its temperature is found to be 350K.

At this time (t_1) the body X is connected to a large body Y at atmospheric temperature T_A through a conducting rod of length L, cross-sectional area A and thermal conductivity K. The heat capacity of Y is so large that any variation in its temperature may be neglected. The cross-sectional area A of the connecting rod is small compared to the surface area of X. Find the temperature of X at time $t = 3t_1$.

The problem seems reasonably complex at first glance, at least to me. So, your first instinct in these cases should be to immediately draw the problem. Here is a rough sketch of the problem:

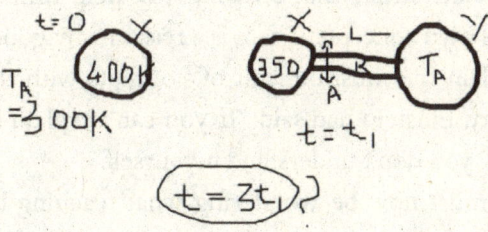

As soon as you draw the problem, you will find you are thinking better and moving faster towards the solution.

The catch is to not overdo it. So don't start taking out scales and compasses and protractors for drawing problem representations. You should be skilled in drawing approximate representations of problem situations. This includes being able to represent distances in relative terms and angles in absolute terms. For example, if there are two rods of 3m and 6m length at 30° angles to each other, your drawing should be able to show that the latter rod is roughly double the former while your angle should be as close to the real 30° as possible. Finally, the drawing is meant for you, not for some art gallery.

14. The Whiteboard Test

Teaching is one of the most difficult tasks in this world. It requires one to be thorough with the concept and be ready to take on all possible questions. It is in these questions that the learning lies for a teacher. The more a teacher teaches a concept, the better he becomes at it. This is because the different questions that students ask help him learn and hone his own concepts. There is a reason why good teachers can explain the most difficult of concepts with the utmost simplicity. Einstein had said: 'If you can't explain it to a six-year-old, you don't understand it yourself.'

You must now be wondering what teaching has got to do with preparing for JEE. There is something that I like to call the whiteboard magic. It is the magical transformation that you undergo when you start explaining something using the whiteboard. Once you are in a situation where you are responsible for another's learning, you automatically become more cautious and refined in your thought process. You start to anticipate questions that might be asked and so force your mind to explore a concept in every possible way. You start coming up with different examples to explain a concept and sometimes do a simple experiment just to demonstrate the effect of a scientific principle. Taking on the role of a teacher frees you and helps you develop a more holistic view of a problem or concept. Even so, I have found that taking on the role of a teacher is not always feasible and also not always required, but it is very helpful when you are not sure about a concept. The questions posed by people, which challenge your way of thinking, will give you a great platform to realize your mistakes and get a good grasp of your shortcomings. So, when you are doubtful about something, go to the whiteboard and explain the concept to your friends. Once you start explaining, you will not only crystallize your thoughts but also, suddenly, you will spot your flaws. Your friends will help you by asking questions or pointing out where you are going wrong.

Solving by staring. Another part of the whiteboard magic is what I like to call the 'burning' of the question by staring at it. For this all you need is a whiteboard, a difficult problem and a few markers. Whenever you are stuck at any problem or concept, it's time to hit the whiteboard. Lay out the problem (the free body diagram, the mathematical equation, the geometry of the problem, etc.) and take a step back and stare at it all. Think about what is known to you and what you need to achieve in order to solve the problem. Then think of a flow (what interim steps you might have to take). Then go to the whiteboard and complete one step. Now again take a step back and see whether what you have done is right or wrong. Evaluate if the approach is leading you ahead or merely making you consider unwanted variables. Stare at the problem, stare hard. Just like a jigsaw puzzle, solve one interim part and then evaluate your overall picture. Keep on doing this till you complete the entire flow and have completed the problem (as per your understanding). Now, if it is correct, figure out where you went wrong earlier and how you can make sure that it never occurs again. If you are still wrong, start staring at the steps you took. Stare at every part of the flow and focus. Try and work the problem backwards and see where you might have gone wrong. If you cannot figure out the problem after spending a considerable amount of time on it, borrow a fresh pair of eyes via a friend and ask him for his thoughts. This will help you get his perspective and figure out the flaw in your approach. If your friends can't help you, ask your teachers. DO NOT ERASE the question till you figure out what is wrong. This approach helps you develop a keen eye for each of the interim steps involved in solving a problem and also generally results in a 'wow!' moment when you solve the problem. (Disclaimer: such a whiteboard exercise might result in a few sleepless nights.)

15. Rule of 84: Your Muscle Memory

There is a big difference between the level of studies in class ten and the syllabi of classes eleven and twelve, especially the

JEE syllabus. Be ready to be bombarded with a lot of new concepts in a short time. There will be more formulae and equations than you can remember. You will be expected to put these formulae and concepts to practice right away. Though it will seem a little overwhelming in the beginning, the trick is to focus on one topic at a time and start getting comfortable with the new concepts, formulae and derivations.

While it is not easy to remember the formulae and equations right away, something that I found very useful was writing things down—often repeatedly. The logic was to make these new formulae a part of my muscle memory. I would keep writing the complete formula in any problem that I would solve.[*] This made sure that I was writing the formulae and not just plugging in the numbers and solving questions (though that comes later when formulae become a part of your muscle memory). So, how many times do you have to write a formula? Well, there is a rule of thumb that I follow, to write a formula or a derivation 84 times (hence the 'rule of 84') and it becomes a part of your system. I have no scientific basis for this rule of 84. It is something that one of my teachers told me (there may be some connection with 8.4 million rebirths in Hindu mythology) and I never questioned it. So, there is no Vedic principle insisting that you have to stick to 84. For some of you it may come a little earlier, for some, a little later.

[*] Paras.

The underlying point in this rule of 84 is that you must be sincere while solving problems. Don't just solve problems in your head. Write down the formulae, draw the free body diagrams, draw the benzene ring structures in organic chemistry, draw the angles and triangles in trigonometry. In short, just write all the steps involved in solving a problem (you can gradually move on to solving questions mentally, after you have had sufficient practice and can quickly map out all the intermediary steps involved). So, till you reach a stage where just reading the question is enough for you to mentally list all the steps and formulae involved, keep writing. Make the important concepts and formulae a part of your muscle memory. It will not only make you more comfortable with the formulae but also give you the confidence you need to write the final exam. A lot of extremely smart people who have the flair to solve things mentally falter because in the final exam there is a lot of anxiety and they tend to doubt what they have written. So write, no matter if you do it wrong, you will remember the equation you botched up because you had written it before and it didn't work. The moment there is a conflict between the muscle memory and the analytical brain, you will know something is not right and you will take stock of the problem in the beginning itself.

A caveat: Try to space out repetitions. Eighty-four times doesn't mean that you sit in one go and keep on writing the same thing multiple times. Practise different problems and not the same problem. But when the concepts involved are similar, just derive the formula again instead of reusing it.

16. The English Language

A general command over a language is a must. When the JEE examination started in the 1950s, it had a mandatory English paper. Later it was dropped on grounds of fairness. I know the arguments in favour of this decision, but my personal opinion is that this should be brought back as a mandatory paper. If your English is weak, don't ignore it. If you score in 90s in mathematics and science but score in 60s in English, consider it a warning signal. Work upon it and make sure you improve your English. Most of the best reference books are written in English and to grasp what the author is really trying to say your English has to be good. The right way to work upon language is to make sure you write and speak whatever you read or hear. When you are done reading a paragraph from a book, try to talk to yourself or a friend about what you understood from it. You can also try writing it out in a few words. Another very important method to develop language skills is to never settle for the approximate. Keep looking for the right word and the right expression to say things. Don't say you are feeling hungry when you are starving. Don't say someone is smart if they are cunning. Make sure you try and find the right word and expression each time. A little bit of reading, especially classics by writers like Charles Dickens and Jane Austen, helps a lot.

SET THE HOUSE IN ORDER

17. Night Owls vs Early-Morning Creatures

When should I study—during the day or during the night—is one of the most common questions asked by students. Some of you are night owls who prefer to burn the midnight oil, while some of you get up early and like to get at it in the wee hours of the morning when there is no disturbance. As to which is right and which is wrong—well, there is no one right answer. Each one of you is different and as such cannot be expected to do something that goes against your nature. You have to realize that you have your own peak hours of concentration and are most efficient at a particular time of the day. It is during those hours that you should focus on going through as much of the syllabus as you can.

There is nothing wrong in sticking to a schedule that allows your mind to work at its best. However, you must take into account that JEE is a long and strenuous exam that starts at nine in the morning and ends at five in the evening. It is an exam where you have to be at the top of your game throughout these long hours. You need to train your mind accordingly. You have to make sure that your mind is attentive, alert and responsive during these particular hours. Here are a few guidelines that helped me train my mind* to be attentive during this period of the day:

* Paras.

Never sleep during the JEE examination hours, that is, 9 a.m. to 5 p.m. If you do, the exam day will be harsh on your body and the by the second half you will be struggling to stay awake and keep your mind attentive. It is important to attune your body so that it is ready to handle stress on the day that counts.

Skip the tea and coffee—stick to water. I have often seen people take coffee or tea before or during a long study session. It's good to have a shot of caffeine if it boosts your concentration but often people get dependent on it and get headaches if they don't get their timely fix. You have to take into consideration that on the final day no one will serve you coffee during the exam. Also, coffee and tea cause dehydration, thereby lowering your concentration once their effect wears off. I found water to be a great beverage to keep the mind alert. Frequently sipping water ensures that you don't feel sleepy and stay properly hydrated. Also, taking a break to drink a little water sometimes calms you down and helps you gather your thoughts (especially when you are struggling with difficult problems).

Eat after every couple of hours and eat right. Students often get so engrossed in a subject that they forget about almost everything else including meals. While it is great to have such good concentration, not taking care of your glucose levels results in a decline in your performance. It's a good idea to keep a few fruits on your study desk and a few nuts (walnuts are mind boosters) in your pocket. Take a break after a couple of hours, pick up a fruit and take a stroll. Get some blood circulating and let your mind take a 10–15-minute breather.

18. Optimize Your Time

'It's not the hours you put in your work that count, it's the work you put in the hours.'—Sam Ewing

I have often been asked how many hours one should study each day to crack the IITs. Again, there is no one answer to this. Different people have different styles so what I am going to describe may not be applicable to you. You are free to explore your routine and discover what works best for you. Take this as a guideline and experiment with it till you find the right schedule for yourself.

The Weekday Schedule. I had a simple schedule: ten problems per subject per day for the weekdays.[*] These ten problems would be from the topics that were currently being taught at school or the coaching class. As I progressed through the topic, I made sure that these ten problems became tougher and required the application of concepts I had learnt over the past few weeks. Thankfully, a lot of books are structured so that the problems get harder as you move ahead in the topic and they require greater mental application of a combination of different concepts. This

[*] Paras.

method worked for me as it helped me cement the new concepts that I learnt every day and revise the concepts that I had learnt over the previous weeks. Also, solving problems from every subject meant that I was comfortable with what was going on in both school and coaching class and was never out of sync with any subject. This is particularly important, because if you lose track of a few classes, chances are that you will never be able to catch up, at least in that particular topic.

The Weekend Grind. The weekends were reserved for the star-marked questions (I am referring here to a problem-difficulty grading technique, about which I will talk a little later) from all the previous topics and especially the topics where I was weak. This meant that in week 10, I would have looked at all the star-marked problems over the past nine weeks for each of the three subjects. This is where the real beauty of the star-mark-grading scheme lies. I could revise topics covered over the previous three months in a single weekend. It made sure that I was always ready to take a test from any of the topics that were covered in class over the past few months. It helped me keep the concepts at my fingertips and slowly but surely made them a part of my system. I understand that as you will cover more topics, it will become difficult and more time-consuming to revise all the topics in one weekend. So, if you find it tough to cover all the topics of all the previous weeks, then you can choose the topics that you want to revise and go on in a cyclical manner so that every month you have had at least one look at all the topics for each of the three subjects (believe me, it's not impossible once you start following the star-mark approach).

In class twelve, make sure that each weekend you pick up at least two topics per subject from class eleven and revisit the star-marked problems. This will ensure that you are still comfortable with what you studied the previous year. JEE tests you on concepts across the two years and you can't afford to forget what you learnt in class eleven.

19. Saving Time

Every JEE aspirant, whether from Delhi or Dhanbad, whether smart or stupid, has exactly the same amount of time to complete the examination. It is logical that students who have the ability to save time will, in general, always do better in exams than those who don't. And saving time, much like saving money, is always done in very small parts. You must keep building tools and techniques and shortcuts that help you save time when solving a problem.

The biggest time-saving device in any exam is calculation shortcuts. Many students waste precious seconds converting CGI to SI units, Celsius to Fahrenheit temperatures, multiplying and dividing large numbers, expanding expressions, and so on. Such tasks are peripheral to the problem you are trying to solve and should be done as quickly as possible so you can spend more time in trying to understand and solve the real problem.

Set aside 10–15 minutes every day for practising these skills and timing yourself so you become faster and more accurate in doing them. A stopwatch is a very handy tool for this. For example, how much time does it take for you to convert 135°C into °F? Ideally it should not take you more than 10 seconds. This might even be possible in 4–5 seconds if you practise really hard. These small things create big differences in JEE ranks. I suggest you keep a separate notebook of these shortcuts and keep looking for smart shortcuts that your classmates use.

As for the number of hours that you should spend on study per day, you must be careful that you do not put too much stress on the quantity and that you focus more on the quality of the time that you spend. Efficiency is really important as after a few hours your mental abilities will nosedive and you must stop before you hit this point. You must build your stamina, but you should make sure that you do not reach the point of fatigue. Take sufficient breaks between studying slots and refresh yourself by listening to some music or playing a physical sport (not Playstation or computer games).

20. All Work and No Play Makes Jack a Dull Boy

One cannot overemphasize the fact that a sound mind lives in a sound body. There is life beyond books. There is learning in playgrounds, in music sessions, in dance rehearsals, in the depths of swimming pools, in the fresh air of the hills and in the cold waters of our rivers. Nature is perhaps the best teacher. Remember, as children we were all very inquisitive about every new thing that we saw. We wanted to touch, feel and explore the new experiences and in the process learnt a lot.

This life beyond your classroom plays a major part in shaping your attitude and personality. The more worldly experience you have, the better you will be able to connect with the learning of the classroom. It will improve your ability to talk about any topic with almost anybody. Life is largely a game of confidence and your experiences give you a confidence that you carry with you everywhere, from an examination hall to an official party.

Research has found that participation in activities such as quizzing, learning to play a musical instrument, dancing, etc., sharpens the memory and increases the grasping power of our brain. So go out there, have fun and learning will happen.

21. The Star-Mark Technique

Over the course of the next two years, you will solve thousands of problems. Not every problem will be worth revisiting (such as problems that you got right in your first attempt, without putting in too much effort). However, there will be some problems that will give you a 'wow!' moment and you will want to revisit those when revising a topic. Chances are, though, that you will not be able to find these questions in your piles and piles of problem sheets.

One of the approaches that I followed to make sure I had problems readily available to revise the entire topic quickly was to create a special star-rating-difficulty-level marking system for the problems that I encountered.* Whenever I couldn't solve a problem the first time (unless it was a silly calculation mistake or some other non-conceptual mistake), I would put a star against that question. A star would also be awarded to the solved problems that took me considerable time and effort and made me revisit a few concepts. These star-marked problems became my revision tool for a particular topic.

The next time I revised that topic, I would go though the concepts and do only the star-marked problems. If I couldn't solve a problem the second time around, I would put another star mark against it. And thus every successive failed attempt would mean another star mark against the problem. So, I ended up with problems that sometimes had five stars next to them. This marking system made sure that while revising, I always looked at problems and concepts that I was most likely to goof up. The grading system also helped me cut down my revision time. If I had to do a quick one-hour review, I would read the concepts again and just look at the four- and five-star problems. If I had more time, I would look at the three-, four- and five-starred problems, and so on. It also meant that I was not overdoing things that I was good at and only redid problems that made me revise concepts on which I had slipped

* Paras.

47

up in the past. Such a difficulty-marking pattern is especially useful when you have to revise the entire two-year syllabus towards the end of class twelve.

A caveat: You have to realize that the star-marking scheme is not about remembering problems. It is not about memorizing certain problems and hoping that they show up in the final exam. Do not mark a problem aiming to memorize it; mark a problem because it helps you delve deeper into a concept and helps you refresh your memory.

22. Speak Out Loud

This applies not just to JEE preparation but to all walks of life. When in doubt, raise your hand and ask. There is no bigger disservice you can do to yourself than not asking things you don't understand. Always know that assumptions are the mother of all mistakes. So, do not assume anything; raise your hand and get complete clarity. No matter how stupid you may think you sound, believe me it is stupider to not seek an answer or an explanation right away. Don't fool yourself with the thought that you will figure it out later. You may actually figure it out later but for the rest of the lecture, nothing will make any sense.

You may be wondering why I vehemently advocate the need to clarify doubts as soon as possible. This is because JEE exam questions will test you on multiple concepts at the same time, and if you are not clear about any one concept, chances are you will get stuck somewhere in a problem and then wonder why didn't you clear this doubt much earlier. You will have to let a question go when you had already solved 75 per cent of it. A couple of such problems and your confidence will take a beating that may affect the rest of your performance.

I have often noticed that people feel shy and awkward about asking questions to clarify their doubts because they think that since no one else is asking, the problem must be trivial. However, it is *you* who is going to write the exam and you have to get your head around all the concepts. Don't worry about what others may think; forget that they may laugh at you. The cardinal rule of the exam is—each for himself. Just raise your hand and ask. Ask your teachers, ask your friends, ask whoever you think can help. Everybody has a unique style of explaining stuff and you must explore all avenues until you are confident about a concept.

If you think that the lecture room may not be the right place to clear your doubts, seek time from your teachers, go to them after the lecture and seek clarification. You could also get clarification from your friends if they are reliable and studious. Do not keep it hanging till the next day or the next week. Also, it is a great practice to go home and do a quick look-through the lecture notes to see if your understanding of the concept (after you have sought clarity on your doubts) is correct.

A caveat: Ask questions when someone is explaining the fundamentals of concepts to you, but don't ask them for solutions to questions. There is a difference between seeking clarification for doubts and expecting to be spoon-fed answers.

23. Post-mortems Know What Prescriptions Don't

Failure is a great teacher for it often teaches you more than any of your victories. However, this is contingent on whether you are willing to give yourself a chance to learn from the failure or you prefer to forget about it and keep moving on as if nothing had happened.

One of the best ways to identify where you fail is to write exams. So, whether you join a coaching class or not, my suggestion is that you certainly join a test series. The reason for this is twofold. One, it gives you a chance to keep on testing your preparation at the national level. Second, it is a great opportunity to fine-tune concepts and find areas where you falter more frequently.

Personally, I feel that the second reason is the most important benefit of any test series. It gives you a chance to understand your weaknesses and work on them. But it seems that this benefit is usually the one that is overlooked. Students do not always put in much effort to analyse the test after they step out of the examination centre. You may have done well overall but a test is useless if you don't use it as a tool to improve your weaknesses. Analysing mistakes after an exam is something that doesn't come naturally to most people—at least to me it didn't.[*] I wanted to relax and not think about the exam or studies the moment I stepped out of the examination

[*] Paras.

hall. I used to be glad that the exam was over and hence my general tendency was to wait for a few days to analyse where I had gone wrong. More often than not that day never came. This was something that cost me at least one question in the final JEE exam (which easily translates into a few hundred ranks). I recognized the question and I remembered coming across it in one of the tests and I knew I had not solved it correctly back then. But, the fool that I was, I hadn't bothered to check the right method to solve that problem. And there was a kick in my guts right in the examination hall. You don't want to be in a situation when the second question you see is one you know you should have cracked in 30 seconds because you have seen it before (a rare possibility) but cannot solve it because you just never bothered to find the right approach. This will throw you off balance and lower your confidence.

So, as a rule never postpone the post-mortem of the exam. Take that answer key, get together with your friends and discuss the questions on your way back home. This will help you discover your mistakes not only by looking at the answer key but also with inputs from your friends. Thomas Edison had said: 'I have not failed. I've just found 10,000 ways that won't work.' Make sure you use each of the tests to learn a way that doesn't work so that when the final day arrives you have exhausted most ways that don't work and are left with only those that do.

GET THE RIGHT TOOLS

24. Concept Sheet

Over the next couple of years you will come across a large number of topics in each of the three subjects—physics, chemistry and mathematics. You will find yourself moving from one big topic to another within a few weeks. The pace will sometimes be mind-boggling and you will find yourself a little lost amidst the progression from one law of motion to another law of differentiation. Also, the use of concepts will cut not only across topics but also across subjects. Physics will require mathematical concepts like differentiation and integration. Your physics teacher will expect your maths professor to teach you about these relevant concepts and will not spend much time explaining them in depth. And in between there will be various weekly, monthly and sometimes daily tests to study for. I am sure you will find yourself wondering when, between all the school classes, coaching classes, sports and exams, will you be able to find the time to study and make sense of what is happening. You require a quick-fix solution, one that gives you a simple synopsis of the different concepts within a topic and tells you how and when to use them. The piece of paper that lets you bring some sanity and order into an otherwise busy and hectic life is what I call the 'concept sheet'.

The concept sheet in its basic form is a concise collation of all the concepts in a topic and shows you how the learning from one concept flows to another forming a logical chain of thought. A concept sheet lays down all the rules and principles of a topic and helps you get a complete overview of the topic in less than 20 minutes. Now to the all-important question: How do you make a really good concept sheet? A good concept sheet starts on the first day of a new topic and ends on the last day of the topic. You start by putting in all the new concepts that you have learnt in a day on the sheet. Every day you add new lessons to the sheet. Keep rereading what you have previously written and prune the unwanted detail to make the sheet crisp and to the point. A good concept sheet will follow the flow of your lectures and keep building upon old concepts. Make sure that you add diagrams and other graphics in a concept sheet so that you can quickly relate to the concepts. Another point to note is that formulae in concept sheets should be written in complete form and not in any shorthand. Just think of a concept sheet as something that anyone can read to get comfortable with the subject.

Now, what makes a concept sheet great is linking it to the specific problems that gave you an 'aha!' or 'wow!' moment. Every time you read a new concept, you will come across problems that will give you a great and in-depth understanding of the concept. These are what I call the 'aha!' moment problems. Make sure you scribble these problems on the margins of your sheet so that a mere glance at it will take you back to the same 'aha!' stage and ingrain the concept deep inside your mind.

While revising a topic, the best approach is to read the concept sheet first and then begin with the star-marked questions. And while preparing for any exam (monthly, weekly, etc.) it is not a bad idea to start revising the concept sheets (as time permits) in reverse chronological order. This will make sure that in every exam you are prepared with the most current concepts from all the topics.

25. Charts

Charts should be all over your study room. Charts are a very nice way to keep revising things on the go. You may be listening to music, talking to a friend, playing computer games or just exercising or walking about in your room. While doing any of these activities, you can always casually look at the charts in your room, which contain key concepts like the periodic table, elementary particles, trigonometric ratios, combinatorial rules, etc. Of course you should not overdo it. You have to wisely select the concepts or topics for which it makes the most sense to create charts. Charts should be made for a scheme of concepts where a table or a graph can be made; and for things that are prone to be confused or forgotten, especially by you. The best examples are trigonometric ratios and the periodic table. In general, whenever you find a topic that has a schema of concepts or values that you keep forgetting or mixing up all the time, it is a good idea to make a chart for it. Also, making charts is quite effort-intensive. So, it is good to share the burden in a study group and then copy the same set of charts within the entire group.

26. Stickies for the Non-sticky Stuff

Post-its are perhaps one of the best inventions of the past century. Nothing can be a better reminder than a Post-it note at the side of your desk. These stickies can be of great help to those preparing for JEE and other competitive exams. You can use the stickies in two ways:

Schedule reminders. As you juggle school homework, lab work, school and test series exams and extracurricular activities, all at the same time, it is very easy to lose sight of the goal and drift from one thing to another. Doing this will not only make you feel a little lost but you will also prevent you from giving your 100 per cent to anything you do. It is really important to maintain focus and concentrate on one thing at a time. You can use Post-it notes to set some daily targets (make sure that these targets are realistic but also not too easy) and tick them off one by one. This will help you keep track of your goals and feel good when you have completed them. It is generally a good idea to note the expected time against each task. Now, you must understand that some tasks may take longer than expected and some may finish earlier than you had envisaged, and thus the expected time will evolve accordingly. This will help you know the areas where you need to build up your speed and areas where your speed is great but you may have to actually slow down to get higher accuracy. There is generally an 'accuracy versus speed' trade-off and this technique will help you understand it and then work on it going forward.

Stickies for important concepts. Often you will come across concepts and topics that will take their own sweet time to become a part of your system. You will find some things that you will not be able to grasp quickly. Use sticky notes to write these down and paste them along the side of your bed. That way you will ensure that you see them often till they are imprinted in your head. You can also use stickies to flag certain pages of a book that you find interesting and would like to read for revision. You can use colour-coded schemes and pick different-coloured sticky notes to mark specific sections as must-reads, good to read, etc.

27. Nurture Your Note Bank

Over the next two years, you will come across of a lot of textbooks. All authors have different styles of writing and you have to navigate these differences and form your own impressions. Remember, books are written according to how the author sees things; notes are made according to how *you* see them. It is very important for you to see things your way by making your own original notes for every important concept you learn.

When writing notes, try and summarize the concept in a couple of lines. Once you are clear about the crux of the concept, decide the structure and the points first, and then start writing the descriptive text. Remember that the advantage notes have over books is that they have to be read only by the person who wrote them. So, as long as *you* understand what you have written, it's fine. The purpose is to jot down the most important bits legibly and succinctly.

Focus on concepts in your notes, not chapters or pages. They may be the same but not always. For instance, I have seen some of my friends writing notes about boxes, side notes and even appendices!

Never make notes from an open book. Read or hear, and then try writing notes sometime later without anyone or a book around. It forces you to explain in words what you think you know and so the gaps in your understanding become evident. Every chapter or section has two or three core concepts. Identify them and make notes about them first.

There is a special format that worked really well for me: the question–answer format.[*] Write all notes in the form of questions so that at the time of revision you can challenge yourself with those questions and then refer to the notes for answers, if you need to.

Have some coding in your notes. Multicoloured and well-annotated notes, though hard to write, are easy to read. I used a lot of personal icons, like big question marks, smileys, stars, etc., to annotate my notes. That made my notes easier for me to understand as well as fun to write.

The notes should be of multiple hierarchical levels. We used to call them 'notes of notes' and 'notes of notes of notes'. So, there should first be a one-line summary of a

[*] Vivek.

concept, then a five-line detailing and then maybe a one-page detailing. This is not a rule, but this structuring helps you in two ways. First, you can structure your revision cycles into short ones and long ones depending on how much time you have for the revision; and, second, you can also prepare yourself for both short-answer and long-answer formats for the same concept.

Do mention catches and 'gotchas' very clearly in your notes. There are always some common mistakes about each concept and keeping them highlighted is very important so that you consciously watch out for them in trick questions, especially under pressure.

GET THE RIGHT HELP

28. Form Study Groups

A study group is often the best place to get answers and clarification on some of the most difficult concepts or questions that one may encounter. There is power in numbers and this manifests itself in the different strengths that different members of the study group bring to the table. Some members may have a good grasp of some topics while others may find other concepts relatively easy. Each member of the study group will be both teacher and student. Learning from your friends helps you air all your questions (some of which you may shy away from asking in a large classroom) and teaching your friends helps you get a good review of the coursework as well as strengthens your confidence and knowledge of that topic. A good study group helps motivate you to do your bit and contribute constructively. It also gives you a good reality check on where you stand compared to your peers. It will help you identify your weaknesses and the group will provide you enough support to work on these areas.

A group is as good as its members so make sure you choose the participants wisely. Look for peers who do well in the course and seem interested and focused. You have to be careful not to form a study group with someone just because you are friends. You need to make sure that your group does not turn into a place for gossip. Do not form groups with friends if they do not share your passion and determination. It will not only destroy the group dynamics but also create a rift in your friendship.

The ideal size of a group is around four to five people. Larger groups are difficult to manage and there may be a few members who do not contribute much to the group. Smaller groups will not add much value and it is easier to lose focus when there are only two or three people in it.

Forming a study group does not mean you have to meet daily and study only with the group. Make sure that group meetings are a weekly affair (or maybe twice a week) where you go over an agreed agenda. Create an agenda for each study group meet. Set expectations from different members and make sure that each member is contributing and benefiting. Align everybody on the topics that need to be reviewed and assign teaching roles to the members who are more comfortable with these topics.

29. Choose Thy Master with Care

While self-study and natural flair can take you through JEE, a bit of coaching and mentoring can add a lot more focus to your preparation, identify your weaknesses and sharpen your skills to suit the JEE needs. Coaching can come from various sources such as an elder sibling who has gone through the paces of JEE preparation, your schoolteachers or specialized JEE coaching centres. The selection of a coach is the biggest decision you have to take when you start thinking of preparing for JEE. Some purists scoff at this idea of coaching, but we all know that to be a top-notch sportsperson you need an awesome trainer. JEE is like a sports event because performance is relative. In that exam hall even though all of you will be sitting in your chairs, in your minds you will be racing against each other to complete the maximum number of questions correctly within the allotted time.

But then, which coaching do you choose? There are two types of coaching institutes—the corporatized factories and the customized workshops. We all know the corporate names in coaching: you will see their full-page advertisements in newspapers, on huge hoardings all over the city, and some of them also appear on TV now. The customized workshops are your local teachers, famous and revered in local circles. Usually, you choose according to where your friends are going because, ultimately, the study group or the friend circle is the most important asset in your JEE preparation days. My advice is to go for classroom courses in a customized workshop and back it up with a correspondence course from a corporate. Also, the customized workshop has to be logistically feasible, that is, as close to your home or school as possible so you don't waste too much time travelling. Make a decision that is right for you and then nudge your group to go there. Don't let the group dictate the coaching to you.

RESPECT THE SYLLABUS

Every relationship in the world has a contract, tacit or explicit. Your relationship with any competitive exam is governed by a very well-written contract called the syllabus. The more professionally conducted the exam, the more important the syllabus. In the four or five pages of the JEE syllabus, the examiners convey very clearly what they expect from you. All you need to do is diligently imbibe each and every word of it and ensure that you live up to those expectations. The previous year's papers do have a role to play but that is more to understand the weightings, that is, how the different parts of the syllabus are marked. Not a word of the syllabus is to be taken lightly. JEE examiners take great care in writing the syllabus down. So, you must take great care in reading it and make sure that you have covered each and every word of it. Anything that is in the syllabus is fair game; never listen to anyone who says that something in the JEE syllabus is not all that important.

30. Physics Syllabus

Let's start with the physics syllabus of JEE 2012. It is divided into six main parts—general, mechanics, thermal, electromagnetism, optics and modern. Now pick up JEE Physics 2012 Paper 1. Each question there can be mapped on to one topic or another within a section of the syllabus. Electricity and magnetism turn out to be the examiners' favourites with eight out of twenty questions from this section. The next most prominent is mechanics with six questions. All the other sections have one or two questions each. Even within mechanics, you can pin down each question to a specific topic. For example, the third question is on uniform circular motion, the nineteenth on the moment of inertia, etc. Hence, every single minute of your JEE preparation should be precisely along the lines of the syllabus. Whenever you are reading a book or solving a problem, you should be aware of the topic of the JEE syllabus that you are working on. It has to become a habit. Only then will you be able to optimize the investment of your time. Never digress from the syllabus.

31. Chemistry Syllabus

Chemistry (especially organic chemistry) is like a vast sea of knowledge in which drowning is a high possibility. There are just too many reactions and colours of compounds and exceptions for you to memorize. There was a time when the JEE syllabus was different from the NCERT (National Council of Educational Research and Training) syllabus. Students focusing on IIT would study only the JEE syllabus and not worry too much about the class twelve syllabus prescribed by NCERT or CBSE (Central Board of Secondary Education). This meant that they would read a lot of books (sometimes just specific sections from specific books). However, with the recent changes in the marking scheme and an attempt by the ministry of human resource development (HRD) to take away the focus from coaching classes, a lot of emphasis has now been placed on the NCERT syllabus. The JEE syllabus now adheres to the NCERT syllabus and the exam does not veer outside it. Thus, it is really important to understand the *scope* of the syllabus.

Go through the detailed syllabus on the JEE website and make sure you do not spend time on things that are not part of it. I have found that the recent NCERT books for inorganic chemistry are very well written and cover the concepts well. If you want to venture out and experiment with other books, make sure you ask your professors and teachers to tell you what is important from the point of view of attempting the JEE and what chapters you should completely ignore. It will save you a lot of time and effort. Stick to only a few books as you just cannot go through them all. Also make sure that these books are of high quality and not randomly picked out from the thousands that hit the market every year.

32. Mathematics Syllabus

The mathematics syllabus consists of algebra, trigonometry, geometry, calculus and vectors. The main topics in algebra are complex numbers, quadratic equations, series and progressions, probability and matrices. Trigonometry is about ratios and their properties. Geometry becomes analytical geometry at this level. Curves are described by equations and you are required to reach spatial conclusions based on algebraic solutions. The parabola, ellipse and hyperbola are the more exotic topics and the locus generalizes all of analytical geometry. A little bit of 3D geometry is thrown into the mix. Calculus has the twins of differential and integral calculus. And, finally, vectors is more like modern physics: you are tested on its basics so you know what's coming your way in your engineering education.

33. The Information Super Highway

We live in the age of the Internet—the world of Google, Wikipedia, e-books, forums and networks. With all this now accessible on a small screen that fits in our pockets, we are all literally on an information super highway all the time. Double that up with all those benign and malignant advisers around you in the shape of friends, relatives, professors, teachers, who will recommend a new book, guide or question bank to you every day. On this super highway the JEE syllabus is your lane. Keep driving in that lane and don't steer too much right or left no matter what.

Let's take an example. You want to read about Newton's laws. For JEE you should stick to the H.C. Verma and the Halliday-Resnicks. But if you go roaming freely on the Internet, read too many entries on Wikipedia, surf around too many forums, you might end up in the warm embrace of Feynman lectures and Goldstein's classical mechanics. You might also get tempted into quantum mechanics and metaphysics. And, mind you, all this is so interesting and so much fun (if you the real JEE type) that you won't even mind the extra hours invested in getting through it all.

However, this is at the cost of your valuable hours. Always remember that the hours you have at hand in a day are an exact and invariable twenty-four. So, while going into deeper waters may be a good diversion, it keeps you from swimming further ahead. Ensure that whenever you read anything, you have a very clear topic from the syllabus in mind and, if possible, a very specific set of JEE problems that will get solved by reading that topic. If there is none, you ought not to be reading it.

LEARN RIGHT

Academic guidance can be provided to you only by experts who communicate through books, classroom teaching or coaching. The scope and intention of this book is not to substitute that in any way but to complement it by giving you direction and additional types of guidance.

I will go parallel to the JEE syllabus by topic but not necessarily in the same order. This is entirely my perspective on these theories and concepts and I am sure that in some cases your or your teachers' understanding could be different and sometimes even better.

My treatment of the topics will:

1. Emphasize core concepts and ideas critical to the subject
2. Offer alternative and intuitive representations of such concepts to aid your understanding of them
3. Provide you with suggested structures and approaches to solving problems.

PHYSICS

34. Concepts, Laws and Constants

Concepts, laws and constants are the three basic elements to solving any physics problem. Once you have complete command over these, you can apply your comprehension, analysis and calculations to the solution. I would strongly suggest to every JEE aspirant to create a self-written handbook of concepts, laws and constants. Force, momentum, energy, specific heat, refraction, resonance, capacitance, etc., are all concepts. Newton's Laws of Motion, Ampere's Law, Biot–Savart Law, Faraday's Law, etc., are all laws. Speed of light, gravitational constant, pi, Boltzmann constant, gas constant, etc., are all constants. Such a handbook should be like a pocket dictionary which you can refer to whenever in doubt or when revising, and the format works exceedingly well for physics.

35. Proportionality and Directionality

Some students tend to get consumed by the sheer number of formulae in physics. There are numerous physical quantities, so many laws and equations to calculate them and tons of constants with odd values and strange dimensions that the whole thing seems overwhelming. Actually, calculations are the easier part of studying physics. Rest assured that those who set the question paper of JEE are smart enough to set up problems in such a way that you will not have to do complex calculations. Lots of steps will tend to cancel each other out and the final calculations would be rather simple. But, in the quest for calculations, students tend to overlook the more important part of physics, which is the proportionality and directionality of physical quantities.

Without even having to calculate the value of physical quantities, you should be able to figure out their proportionalities and directionalities. For example, when two people jump off a cliff, it should be immediately evident that both will fall downwards (direction), that both will reach the ground at the same time (proportionality) and that the heavier person will probably face more air resistance when falling due to his larger size and not due to his weight. Similarly, when a current-carrying loop is placed in a magnetic field, the most important things to know are that when the current is parallel to the direction of the magnetic field the force is zero, when it is at an angle the force is proportional to the sine of the angle and that the direction of the forces follow the right-hand-curl rules.

You should be in the habit of drawing quick graphs connecting two physical quantities in a situation, which is far more important than calculating their values. As the temperature of an ideal gas increases, it is most important to first establish that the pressure will increase in direct proportion to the temperature if the volume is kept constant. You should be able to quickly draw a graph connecting pressure and temperature. Finding the exact value of the pressure for a given temperature and conversion into the correct units is the easier part of the problem. Statements like 'as X increases linearly, Y decreases exponentially' should become second nature to you.

36. The Ideal World

You will hear the word 'ideal' a lot in physics. It is always going to be something that is impossible and never happens. Frictionless surfaces, ideal gases, infinite surfaces, zero-gravity planets, point-sources of light, and so on. Why do we talk about such things when they can never exist in the real world? Well, because it is always a good way to start! Making assumptions and accepting ideal conceptualizations is a very important habit to develop in physics. It is the fundamental method for solving problems in physics. You first simplify a problem by making assumptions and using ideal concepts. Once you solve that, you introduce realities one by one and modify the problem. This way, you can reach an almost accurate solution in minimal time and get an approximate idea of what is going on. If you start with all the complexities at once, you will take ages to solve the complete problem. So, ideals and assumptions are a necessary and very useful part of the world of physics and you must learn to appreciate their merit and habituate yourself to them.

Mechanics

Once you have got into the habit of being steadfast to the syllabus, you should then get into the practice of prioritizing the allocation of your time and energy. After a detailed analysis of all the JEE papers, I have arrived at a list of the relative importance of the various topics and sections. Clearly, mechanics and electricity-magnetism are the examiners' favourites. Why? Because these topics lend themselves very well to trick questions with a lot of moving, interacting parts. So many interesting problems can be woven using the numerous basic concepts and equations that it becomes an examiner's delight. A separate word of caution about mechanics is in order here. Some students tend to mistake all of JEE physics to be just mechanics; they obsess over it, solve too many problems from too many textbooks and still find that the JEE presents them with problems that are unique and difficult, year after year. What is this mystery behind mechanics? Mechanics is the closest to everyday life. It is the most intuitive of all branches of physics. It allows your imagination to run wild. So, while you must master it, you must not let it master you.

Take a reality check whenever you are doing mechanics—are you overdoing it? There could a sphere rolling off an incline which is placed on a moving car that is running on a road defined by a trigonometric function, and you can go into tortuous folds just trying to work out when that damn sphere will hit the road. But is every such new (and purposely convoluted) problem in mechanics adding value to your quiver of core concepts? Let me assure you that any ordinary physicist can cook up remarkably complex mechanics problems for you in no time. Tuition centres and practice-book writers can so easily make your life hell in mechanics that you won't believe it. After a while it just becomes like a game of Angry Birds where you can keep playing level after level, patting yourself every time you earn three stars, but skill-wise you don't improve at all. The really useful questions in mechanics are those that reveal something new to you. After every mechanics problem that you solve you should ask yourself, did I learn some new concept? So, as long as it's a sphere and an incline on earth, it is more or less the same. But the moment the sphere is made hollow instead of solid, then we are talking! A new concept of moment of inertia is now to be grasped, and that takes you a step ahead.

37. Objects, Systems and Frames

Let's say there is a cart carrying a bucket with two balls inside the bucket. What are the objects, systems and frames of reference here? The intuitive answer is four objects, one system and one frame of reference. This one would say from the immediate picture that comes to the mind, of you standing on the roadside with the cart passing you by. But you have to learn to think a little differently. What if you were a fly? Now, as a fly, you could sit inside the cart, you could sit inside the bucket or you could even sit on one of the balls. Then the world would appear differently to you, would it not? Try and visualize it. This is the skill you have to acquire—to be able to see a system from different points of view, to be able to see and solve a system from different frames of reference. A frame of reference is one of the most important concepts in physics. In *every* mechanics situation that you are faced with, the *first* thing to think about should be your frame of reference.

Even the number of objects that you *see* can change. In the example above, you could possibly take the bucket and the two balls together as one object and solve whatever the posed problem was. You could also take the cart, the bucket and the balls together as one object. Why and how would you do it? You would do this to make your life easier. For example, if a wind was blowing and you were required to predict the motion of the cart under the influence of the wind, you probably wouldn't want to worry about the bucket and the balls separately. Just add the mass of the bucket and the balls to the mass of the cart and solve your equations. You have to bring in the concept of centre of gravity (CoG) and you can easily do this. CoG allows you to make objects out of systems and hierarchically structure a system into subsystems. It is much like a bagful of oranges. If all you are required to do is to lift it, you just need to worry about the one full bag; but if you are required to bang it into the ground and then figure out where all the oranges would land, you will have to worry about each orange separately.

In a nutshell, then, you must learn to see a system from different frames of reference (as a fly) and consisting of different number of objects (using CoG). You do all this to make a problem easier to solve. Here is a tip: make the best use of frames of reference to calm a system down. So in the example above, when you sit on the road, too many objects are moving around. But when you sit inside the cart, suddenly everything *calms* down. For this reason alone, frames of reference are usually attached to CoGs as CoGs are most likely to be stationary in a system. Ultimately, it is an art to look at a problem with an optimal set of CoGs and frames of reference. It could make a huge difference to the time taken to solve a problem if these are not carefully chosen. It could save you valuable minutes of computation and steps (sometimes even hours!) if you develop the art of seeing the best frame of reference from which to solve a problem. In fact, you can change the frame of reference for different parts of the same problem or system. Try it, it's great fun!

38. Dimensions and Coordinates

Any problem in physics is stated within a certain number of dimensions and is solved within a certain set of coordinates. Unless you are really clear in your head about these two things, you are very likely to go astray when solving problems. Let's take for example Question No. 2 in the Physics Screening paper of 2003.

What is the maximum value of the force F such that the block shown in the arrangement does not move?

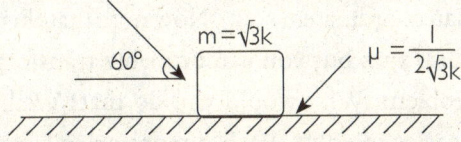

For a moment don't worry about the solution or the options. Just answer this—how many dimensions is this problem stated in and what set of coordinates would be used to solve it?

Clearly, in this case the answer is two dimensions and two-dimensional (2D) Cartesian coordinates (x,y). It is not difficult in this case to identify these; but it is still very important. This should become a habit.

Consider another slightly more involved example from the 1997 Physics Mains paper:

A cart is moving along x direction with a velocity of 4 m/s. A person on the cart throws a stone with a velocity of 6 m/s relative to himself. In the frame of reference of the cart the stone is thrown in y-z plane making an angle of 300 with vertical z axis. At the highest point of its trajectory the stone hits an object of equal mass hung vertically from a branch of a tree by means of a string of length L. A completely inelastic collision occurs in which the stone gets embedded in the object. Determine . . .

How many dimensions? Which coordinates?

The answer is three dimensions and three-dimensional (3D) Cartesian coordinates (x,y,z). Now note that this problem is stated in 3D/x,y,z but you can probably transform it into a 2D/x,y problem. Why would you do that? Well, because it makes it easier to solve. Each dimension in a system is a separate problem to solve. In a 2D system, you have two problems to solve, in a 3D system you have three problems to solve. So, fewer the dimensions, fewer the problems to solve!

The following methods should make your life easier:

1. *Reducing the number of dimensions in a problem.* You should try and reduce 3D problems to 2D and 2D to 1D. You should at least know how to. In the problem above, if you sit inside the cart, it might become a 2D problem.

2. *Aligning the system to the right set of coordinates.* Try and align the coordinates along the paths of motion of the majority of the objects in the system. For example, if a

system has most of the objects moving in circular fashion, it might be best to use angular coordinates. If objects are largely moving in a linear fashion in two dimensions, Cartesian 2D coordinates would be better suited.

39. Vectors

This is the one of the first non-intuitive barriers to cross in your JEE journey. A vector is something that has both magnitude and direction. Well, that is just the textbook definition. You must take the time to assimilate this idea. Unless your mind accepts this you will always be in trouble. Honestly, vectors are just a shortcut in mathematics to be able to say two things at the same time. So, in class six you would have said the train is moving north at a speed of 100 kmph. But in class eleven you say the same thing by stating that the train has a velocity of 100^l. It is just a smarter, shorter and standard way of saying the same thing. You have to learn this new language. It is like the English thriller movies where FBI agents talk to each other using terms like 'Roger that' instead of 'Yes, that is right', or 'Copy that' instead of 'Yes, I heard you', etc. By agreeing to talk to each other in a standard—coded, if you will—language we save time and energy. Vectors are part of this mathematical language that you learn where you can communicate about the exact magnitude and direction of something in a standard, unambiguous way.

Ideas like angular velocity being perpendicular to the plane of motion because it is a cross product, that the dot product of two vectors is a scalar, etc., are things that are a little annoying in the beginning because you are asked to accept these at face value with no 'Whys' allowed. Make sure you ask your teachers about vectors till your mind accepts these as a new way of life. There is a little bit of learning and a little bit of unlearning involved here. You have to unlearn the way you used to think about certain things in junior classes and learn new ways of thinking and speaking about the same things. It will take time and you must give it that time.

40. Forces and Motion

A long time ago a gentleman named Aristotle observed that anything that moves must have some force acting on it. So, a ball will move only when some force is applied to it. Without force everything would remain in a natural state of *rest*. Almost 2000 years later, another gentleman named Galileo Galilei corrected him and added that everything would either remain at rest or *in a constant state of motion* unless a force acts on it. The key was to equate rest with constant state of motion. Aristotle missed it because he hadn't thought of friction! This was such a significant observation that after this it took about a mere fifty years for Sir Isaac Newton to publish his famous *Laws of Motion*, which stood firm and unchallenged for the next 300 years. (Of course, then a certain Albert Einstein came in and spoiled the party. Ever since, we are all just chasing the Higgs boson to be able to meaningfully complete an incomplete theory called Quantum Mechanics.)

An important point to note is that it took mankind 2000 years to understand (and accept) that motion at constant velocity is equivalent to being at rest. I am surprised that JEE aspirants accept this definition in less than two minutes! A system is said to be changing its state *only* when it accelerates in some way; and there are two and only two mechanical ways for acceleration—change in magnitude of velocity or change in direction of velocity, because velocity is a vector. Finally, anything that brings about such change in a system is called Force.

Please spend some time understanding that constant velocity and rest are the *same* thing in physics. You can make a system moving at constant velocity appear to be in a state of rest if you see it from a frame of reference that is moving at the same constant velocity. Such frames are also called inertial frames. Frames that are accelerating are called non-inertial frames. In non-inertial frames you will always have to invent at least one fictional force to fully explain the motion of the bodies within that frame.

Equilibrium

Force does not always cause change in a system. There could be a state when multiple forces operating on a system in a given frame of reference cancel each other out and the state of the system is left unchanged. Say it out loud with me— 'Change is Acceleration'. Such a system that is not changing is in equilibrium. A train moving at constant velocity, even if moving at 100 kmph, is in equilibrium. Only when it speeds up, slows down or makes a turn does it go out of equilibrium.

Equilibrium itself could be along just one dimension among many in a system. For example, in a 3D Cartesian system, there could be equilibrium along the x and z axes but not along the y axis. As emphasized earlier, you have to look at each dimension separately and independently of other dimensions. Static and dynamic equilibrium are much less important, because, as the great man Galileo clearly said, there is no difference between rest and constant velocity motion, at least in the laws of physics.

Angular Motion

Do you know how many new concepts you are introduced to when you move from linear to angular motion when studying physics? ZERO! Yes, everything in angular or circular motion is just a corresponding special case of all the basic laws of linear motion. For velocity there is angular velocity; for x,y,z there are r, θ, φ; for momentum there is angular momentum; for force there is centrifugal force, and so on. The most important thing you have to understand is that angular motion is nothing but everything you already know about mechanics from linear motion, applied to bodies moving on circular paths.

'Why is it so important then?' you may ask. 'Why not study square motion or trapezoidal motion?' Well, unfortunately, that's how God decided to make the universe. Most of the things that matter in the universe are circular or roughly circular in shape. What goes around comes around—don't they say that about life? That's why it is very important for students of physics to be able to apply the laws of angular motion and solve problems in angular dimensions. You could of course apply the basic laws of linear motion to solve angular-motion problems; in fact, learning some additional concepts in angular motion actually gives you handy shortcuts so you can quickly solve angular-motion problems.

Mastery in angular motion comes from a mastery over angular coordinates and vectors. If you can handle these mathematically, you won't face any problems in angular motion.

Gravity

If you understand orbits and escape velocity, you don't need to worry at all about the problems related to gravity, planets, satellites, etc. Just make sure you know very clearly what a geostationary orbit is, what apogee and perigee are and what escape velocity is. The value of g also comes in handy at times. These are the only new concepts in this domain. Everything else is just about solving problems in angular motion, which you already know very well. If examiners throw in a question in this area, it will usually be a dolly and you should just watch out for silly mistakes.

The laws of gravitation and the so-called gravitational field are just special cases of the laws of motion and kinetic and potential energy. Don't waste too much time on these problems.

41. Momentum and Energy

Before I talk about momentum and energy in mechanics, I want to talk a bit about momentum and energy in the JEE preparation itself. I have seen many students try to cover topics quickly as though it were a race. They keep discussing how much of the syllabus they have *covered* and how this person is ahead of that one in *coverage*. Scary stories are spread about 'student ninjas' who have already 'reached energy' while ordinary people are still 'on force'. Do not get carried away by this rat race to finish topics without understanding them. The learning curve in physics is a step function, not a straight line. People who divide time by topics, and try to build a linear curve for their learning, end up like the straight line in the graph shown opposite. They may initially look to be moving fast but finally end up short of the complete depth required to crack the JEE. One the other hand, students who give each topic its due time end up much higher on the curve.

Before delving into momentum and energy you should be really sure that you have understood dimensions, coordinates, frames, CoG, vectors and force correctly. Before we even begin to talk about these two, we have to talk about the class of problems that vectors, etc., help the most in solving. These are collision problems.

Force brings about gradual changes in the state of a

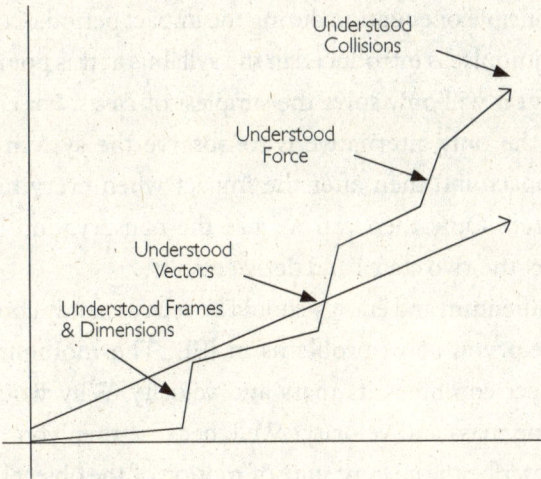

system. It can make objects in a system move faster or slower. Collisions, on the other hand, bring sudden change. Collisions are events that suddenly change the state of a system with multiple objects. Force and frames of reference alone cannot help you when collisions happen. You then need momentum and energy and the conservation laws. Conservation laws of momentum and energy help you connect the different states of a system that are separated by a collision.

Let me explain this in greater detail. In the above example of the cart with the bucket and balls, you can always determine the speed of the cart when it is pushed by a certain force, you can figure out the angle at which the bucket will tilt given certain masses and friction coefficients, and so on. But what if the cart hits a wall? That impact and the change it brings about in the system is so sudden that it is not feasible to apply any principle or equation during the impact period. A concept called impulse is introduced in the syllabus at this point to aid you, but it will only solve the simplest of cases. For complex cases, the only alternative is to observe the system before the impact and then after the impact when everything has stabilized. Only then can we use the conservation laws to connect the two states and derive results.

Momentum and energy should be seen as handy constructs that help you solve problems in JEE. The momentum of an object combines its mass and velocity. Why would you combine mass and velocity? Well, because then you can not only describe the current state of motion of the object but also tell how it will interact with and respond to other objects and forces. Again, like velocity, you are saying two things in one number. So, if you want to know the difference in effort it will take to stop a paper plane flying at 100 kmph and a real plane flying at 100 kmph, all you need to know is their momentum. The greater the momentum of an object, the more the force required and the greater the impact when it hits other objects.

Energy is more intrinsic to objects than momentum. It is the scalar that rules over all vectors in mechanics. Energy is probably the most widely used quantity in physics and yet the least understood. Notable physicist Richard Feynman had said this about energy in his highly acclaimed *Feynman Lectures*: 'It is important to realize that in physics today, we have no knowledge what energy is . . . it is just a strange fact that we can calculate some number and when we finish watching nature go through her tricks and calculate the number again, it is the same.'* In a nutshell, then, you cannot really *understand* energy. Accept the fact that it is a number that oddly remains conserved and constant, and move on and use it when solving problems, without worrying too much about what it really means. Of course, the various types of energy and their formulae is something you will learn as part of your preparation and I won't go into that. All I want to emphasize is that *energy is a number that can be calculated about any object or system, that this number stays constant through any process and that this property of this number is very useful when solving problems in mechanics*.

So, here's what to keep in mind—conservation laws, of both momentum and energy, help you in collision situations. Energy is the most important and least understood concept in all of physics.

42. Moment of Inertia

What is the difference between rotation and revolution? Consider the solar system. There are two ways of looking at it—either that the planets are individually *revolving* around the sun or the solar system as a whole is rotating about its centre of gravity. This is once again the 'centre of gravity and frame of reference' concept. Rotation and revolution are nothing but two ways of looking at uniform circular motion. The

* Richard Feynman, Robert B. Leighton and Matthew Sands, *Feynman Lectures on Physics, Vol. 1* (California: California Institute of Technology, 1964).

concept that allows you to convert a rotation problem into a revolution one, and vice versa, is moment of inertia. So, what you essentially do is encapsulate all the complexity of various small revolutions into a single number called the moment of inertia and then look at the system as a rotating system.

Here is a key problem that I was once asked, which helped me understand the concept of moment of inertia: you are given two spheres, one hollow and one solid. They look exactly the same from the outside and weigh exactly the same. How would you find out which one is solid and which hollow? Now, this is a problem that is oriented towards the configuration of a rigid body in terms of the *distribution* of the individual particles that make it up. In the hollow sphere they are all close to the surface, while in the solid one they are evenly distributed from the surface to the core. The only difference between them will be their moments of inertia.

43. Harmonic Motion and Waves

How much time have you spent playing with a spring in your childhood? How many times have you played with a pendulum as a kid? And how often have you actually seen a *wave* (waves from the sea don't count)? This part of mechanics is not so readily encountered in daily life and hence is intuitively a little distant. But, trust you me, the examiner is in the same shoes. The best part about harmonic motion and waves is that the topic is so limited in scope (at least in the JEE syllabus) compared to linear and angular motion that the trickiness of the questions that can be framed on it is also very limited.

In all harmonic motion situations there will be some kind of a constant called the elasticity constant or Young's constant or some such thing. This constant tells you the stretching ability of an object or system. In some ways, this is the strength with which a system reacts when it is stretched or compressed. It is a property of the system. The only way to determine this constant is to experimentally measure it. So when you actually pull and release a spring, or attach a mass to it and see it vibrating, only then can you calculate the value of this constant. Even if you are cutting a spring in two or joining two springs together, you can determine the constant only by doing an experiment on the system. It could be a thought experiment, that is, one that you imagine in your head.

Once you understand the nature and importance of this constant, everything else is just the same basics—of frames, vectors, dimensions and forces. All you need is decent mathematical skills to solve harmonic motion problems.

44. Fluid Mechanics

When we are in the domain of solids, the smaller parts of a solid are so tightly bound together that you don't have to worry about them separately. But once you get into the domain of fluids, these particles are a little freer to do their own stuff, leading to more problems for you. They are much like little children—the more liberties you give them, the more problems they create for you!

Let's take the example of pressure. Why is pressure in fluids such a big deal? Solids also exert pressure on each other. After all, isn't pressure just force per unit area? Pressure in fluids becomes an important factor because particles in a fluid are free and hence an object can occupy any place within a fluid. The fluid itself can flow in various shapes and sizes through various channels. A fluid is shapeless and formless! Hence, one has to come up with a generic formula to describe pressure in a fluid, independent of how and where one measures it. So, whether it is in a tube or flowing through a pipe or just standing in a glass, the same formulae can always be used to measure pressure.

Pascal's Law, buoyancy and surface tension are all phenomena that arise because in fluids you have to consider the particles separately as they are loosely coupled. In solids, you are always talking about the one big object or that single particle, but in fluids you are always talking about interactions among and the aggregate behaviour of independent particles. The most-needed skills to excel in fluid mechanics are the understanding and acceptance of fluids as a collection of loosely bound particles and the ability to integrate these when required. So, while earlier you were mostly differentiating things to go from distance to velocity to acceleration, etc., now you will be integrating things so you can combine the behaviour of a lot of particles into a common behaviour.

Note that when studying fluid mechanics, your journey into heat and thermodynamics has already begun. So invest some time in understanding and appreciating the nature of fluids and the interactions of the particles within them.

Viscosity is the measurement of the difficulty that a fluid creates for something moving through it because of the attraction among particles. Think of it like moving through a crowd. Terminal velocity is a derived concept describing the steady state achieved when gravity and viscosity cancel each other out.

And finally, think of Bernoulli's equations and equations of continuity as the conservation laws of energy applied over the aggregate mass of particles in a fluid. Believe me, fluid mechanics is easy! You just need to know these terms and equations, practise by solving a few problems and avoid making silly mistakes when doing the maths.

45. Waves and Sound

This, again, is one of the simplest parts of mechanics so just make sure you get the basic terms, definitions and maths right without making silly mistakes. Waves are created due to interactions among the particles in a system. If you throw a stone in a pond, you are hitting an area on the surface of the pond that contains a certain number of particles. These particles will respond to the stone hitting them. You should visualize these particles as connected by tiny threads to neighbouring particles. Because of these threads the neighbours will get affected, then their neighbours, then theirs, and so on. This coordinated and sequential motion of particles, when seen from the outside, appears to be a wave travelling through the fluid. At times the particles are so small and far apart that one cannot see them with the naked eye, but the phenomenon still occurs.

The key terms related to waves are frequency, amplitude and wavelength. Always think of dense crowds of people when you are working with problems in waves. People keep pushing each other in crowds. The force with which they push determines the amplitude, that is, how hard each person is shaking laterally. The way they are standing and bonded to each other determines the wavelength. So, if they are close and quickly transfer the push to the next person the impact travels swiftly from person to person and the wavelength is short; if they are far apart, the wavelength is longer.

Even the superimposition of waves can be handled intuitively in this way. Let's say there is a queue of people and the persons at the beginning and the end both start pushing with the same force; so, one wave will start from the left and one from the right. The person in the middle will be left standing straight as he is pushed equally from both sides. If you were observing from the outside, you could say that two waves of equal amplitude and wavelength moving in opposite directions have cancelled each other out: as always, just a fancy yet scientifically rigorous way of saying something obvious.

Finally, understand that sound and light are just two special kinds of waves because our bodies are tuned to respond to them in different ways. Our ears respond to sound waves, our eyes respond to light. Certain interesting physical phenomena related to sound waves are resonance, beats and the Doppler Effect. There are very few questions on these topics and you can master them from any simple book. Light waves are so interesting that lenses and mirrors becomes a separate section in your syllabus, so we will come to that later.

Mechanics in Summary

As you will have realized by now, mechanics is the most twisted of all disciplines. It is a lot about problem-solving. The books I personally found the most helpful were those by Resnick & Halliday and the problem book by Igor Irodov. These books come with a 'don't-try-this-at-home' warning. Some of the problems in them can carry you away and their complexity is not something you should necessarily get into. If you are smart enough to know what to skip, these books are highly recommended.

Thermal Physics

Mechanics talks about a small number of large objects at reasonably large distances from each other; thermal physics talks about a large number of small objects, very close to each other. In mechanics, observations are made on individual objects, while in thermal physics observations are never made on individual objects but on a large number of particles. How large is this number? Really large at times! For example, one mole of anything is said to contain 6.023×10^{23} particles of the substance. The total population of the world is only about 7×10^9 people. Thermal physics is all about laws and principles applicable to a large—really large—number of closely interacting particles.

46. Heat and Work

The fundamental interest scientists have in studying thermal physics in such great detail is to figure out how to convert work into heat and vice versa. Imagine an icy-cold river flowing rapidly and a house next to it with no electricity. The owner of the house would really love to have some hot water to bathe in but the river is cold and he has no electricity. What does he do? To heat the river water he needs, well, heat, which is thermal energy. The river has a lot of energy but it is kinetic energy due to its rapid flow. What if we could use the kinetic energy of the river to heat the water in it? This is where physics comes in. If you make the water fall on to a turbine to make it rotate, the rotating turbine is now doing work, which you convert into electricity by using magnetism, and then make the electricity flow through high-resistance material which heats up and then transfers that heat back to the water. You have hot water!

As a concept, work is said to happen only when something moves.

Heat is the amount of excitement in the constituent particles of an object. The more excited the particles are, the hotter the object is. Heat flows from high temperature to low temperature, much like water, which flows from higher to lower levels and seeks to create a uniform level everywhere.

Problems related to heat and heat transfer should be structured as follows:

1. All objects in the system should be identified, including the atmosphere or air.

2. You must then identify for each object their two most important properties:

   a. Their capacity to store heat

   b. Their ability to transmit heat

3. Both storage and transmission of heat are dependent on the single-most important thing in all heat problems— the temperature.

Using these constructs, you should draw the problem and then solve it for the various heat-storage and transmission points. A heat-transfer problem is analogous to a mechanical-motion or electrical-circuit problem. Temperature plays the role of height or potential. Thermal conductivity plays the role of friction or resistance. Heat capacity plays the role of mass or electrical capacitance.

Temperature, in some ways, shows the willingness of an object to give up its heat energy to other objects. It is like talkativeness in a way. Some people cannot hold in the secrets they know. So, they keep talking to other people all the time. How much someone is talking doesn't really measure how much they know. It just measures the extra amount of information that they are unable to keep to themselves and must give away to others. Similarly, temperature does not really measure the energy or heat inside an object. It measures how much of that heat is ready to be given away. So, two objects heated with the same intensity for the same length of time will not end up having the same temperature. One will be able to retain less and will hence be at a higher temperature; the other may absorb more and be at a lower temperature.

47. Heat Capacity

What happens to the heat that is passed on to an object? As mentioned earlier, heat is like excitement. So, the particles of the object get more excited when heated. In their excitement, they want to hop and jump and dance around. If they are not allowed to show their excitement, they get stressed. If we allow them to create more space amongst themselves, their stress levels will be reduced and they will start occupying that extra space. The space that gets created among particles in an object is the volume. The stress that develops among particles in an object is the pressure. The amount of dancing and jumping that the particles are doing is the temperature. Make sure you understand the concepts of pressure, temperature and volume very well before you go deeper into thermal physics.

You can only store something inside an object up to the object's capacity. Heat capacity defines how much heat you can store inside an object. As explained before, temperature is the heat that is ready to overflow from an object because its particles are not able to keep their heat to themselves. So, if the heat capacity is high, temperature will not rise as fast as when the heat capacity is low.

The heat capacity of an object is largely the function of the nature and configuration of its particles. Since the nature and configuration of particles does not change with the size of an object, it is handy to take size out of the equation and define heat capacity on unit mass or unit volume basis. This is what specific heat capacity and molar heat capacities are. So, for a block of aluminium, the specific heat capacity does not change with size because that depends only on the fact that it is aluminium. Only heat capacity changes with size, while specific heat capacity remains same.

One last important point about heat capacity is the concept of constant pressure and constant volume. Think of it like this—lack of space and higher stress always reduces excitement so the amount of excitement generated would not just be a function of who you are but also of how much space and stress you have. Therefore, heat capacity will always depend on pressure and volume. So we have to define two kinds of heat capacities, one at constant pressure and one at constant volume. The two are related and the former is easier to measure.

48. Expansion

Let us say we keep two balls at a one-metre distance from each other. We then move them farther apart, by say another metre.

Is this expansion? No. Because 1) the number of objects is not large enough, 2) the size of the objects is not small enough and 3) the distances between the objects are not small enough. We can only talk of expansion when a large number of small particles very close to each other move uniformly farther apart. When this happens, the object that the particles make up is said to expand.

Expansion can get confusing at times because of the various kinds of expansion, that is, linear, surface and volumetric. It is important to understand that expansion can happen in any direction and the coefficient of expansion fundamentally measures how much something will expand for a unit change in temperature. The actual coefficient of expansion will always depend upon what type of expansion is being talked about.

When solving problems related to expansion, be very clear whether the problem is about linear, surface or volumetric expansion. The examiner will drop enough hints for you to figure it out. Whenever you read words like 'negligible' or 'very small', it is a hint to neglect that dimension. So, if there is a rod whose cross-section area is 'negligible', you have to think only of linear expansion.

49. Processes

Processes are the thermal equivalent of collisions in mechanics. We are very interested in the state of a system before and after certain stimuli are provided to it. We must keep in mind that in mechanical collisions the input is provided over a very small interval of time and the change is instant, while in thermal processes the input is provided over a longer period of time and the change is gradual. The stimulus in mechanical collisions is usually force, while in thermal processes the stimulus could be pressure, temperature or volume. Volume as a stimulus can seem confusing. Think of it this way—you can change the volume available to particles in a system and that is indeed a stimulus. It is fascinating to note that ultimately pressure, temperature or volume, applied at the level of the particles, finally ends up as force that individual particles apply on each other. In thermal physics we are dealing with a large number of small particles and our intention is to solve the entire set as a whole rather than worry about individual particles. Hence we talk only in terms of pressure, temperature and volume, which are concepts applied to a collection of particles.

Now the biggest problem here is that if everything is changing simultaneously in a system, it becomes very hard to track the changes or predict the final state. Pressure, temperature, volume and heat all depend on each other and if all are allowed to change, it will become really hard to determine the final state of a system. So, we first think of ideal situations where only three out of these four are changing at a time, with the fourth held constant. Then we can observe the behaviour of one versus the other two and the best thing we can do is draw graphs on paper to visualize those changes. These various idealizations of processes are known as:

- *Isobaric processes*, when the pressure (historically measured in bars) stays fixed
- *Isothermal processes*, when the temperature stays fixed
- *Isochoric processes*, when the volume (*choros* is Greek for space) stays fixed
- *Adiabatic processes*, when the heat stays constant

In the study of all these processes, we come across lots of equations and charts, and it gets a little confusing. Please note the following:

- There is only one type of diagram that is important for JEE purposes and that is the P-V or pressure-volume diagram.
- The P-V diagram is important because work done by an ideal gas is given as P∆V, that is, pressure times the change in volume. There is some amount of complexity in adding and subtracting different units of work when pressure, temperature and volume change in different ways in a thermodynamic process. Tracing it on a diagram makes it easier.
- The area in the P-V curve gives you the work done.

50. Laws of Thermodynamics

I have already talked about the utility of ideal concepts in Tip #36, 'The Ideal World'. An ideal gas is a theoretical concept of a collection of zero-sized particles that don't interact with each other. Literally, it means nothing, but it beautifully simplifies a lot of equations. The ideal gas law connects the three fundamental measures of a system—its pressure, temperature and volume—in a very simple equation that you can use to arrive at approximate solutions to problems in thermal physics. Of course, the closer the real substance is to the ideal gas assumptions, the better the approximations would be.

The ideal gas law becomes the starting point for a lot of derived equations and principles under special circumstances.

The first law of thermodynamics can be put in layman terms as follows: when someone gives us money, we can either spend it to buy something or save it in our bank account to be used later. Similarly, when we apply heat to something, it can either do work using it, or store it inside itself as internal energy. In fact, the first law is nothing but the law of conservation of energy stated in thermal terms.

Application of the first law requires a very clear understanding of heat, work and internal energy. Heat is money, work is spending and internal energy is saving. How can an ideal gas spend heat as work? When a gas expands, it works against the pressures that were keeping it constrained. Typically, these pressures are applied by pistons. So, when you heat a gas container it will push against the walls of the container. If they move, it has done work. If they don't, the heat is stored in the gas as internal energy.

51. Radiation and Black Bodies

Excess excitation in a system is indicated by temperature and we know that when it finds another system with a lower level of excitation it will pass on heat to the other system and try to reach thermal equilibrium. However, there is a way in which things can get rid of their excess excitation without the need to get in touch with another object—that is radiation. The key concepts here are absorption, emission, reflection and transmission of radiation. *The first key point* to note is that absorption and emission are the opposites of each other so only one of them will be used when relating them to other quantities or in equations. They can never appear together in an equation. *The second key point* is that the sum of absorptivity, reflectivity and transmitivity for a surface is 1. JEE paper-setters usually throw a googly using these concepts and students don't take the topic seriously; this often leads to an unnecessarily lost mark.

That finally leaves us with Kirchoff's, Wien's and Stefan's laws. I am not going to state the laws here as you can find them in any book, but I advise to not neglect them and to understand clearly the distinction and purpose of each. I can assure you there will be a question or two in every JEE paper on black body radiation where one or more of these laws will be used. And I can assure you it is mostly the 'smart' students who get these questions wrong, just because they did not respect the topic enough.

Thermal Physics in Summary

As it goes, you have to 'feel the heat'. Up to now you felt it with a thermometer, now you have to feel it with a microscope.

The most important connect to make is with the underlying world of particles and radiations that finally make something feel hot or cold. Once you build that connect and start to conceptually appreciate thermal physics, you will find it much easier than mechanics. This is also because things cannot be twisted much in thermodynamics. Things get far more complex in the next section.

Electricity and Magnetism

In mechanics we talked about direct interaction between objects. We then went a level deeper and started talking about the properties and interactions among objects due to what their constituent particles do. We will now talk about how objects interact based on what the constituents of their constituent particles, namely electrons, are doing. So we are going deeper and deeper, zooming more and more inside objects to find out more—from objects to particles and now to electrons and protons. Fascinating! Brace yourself, because when we reach modern physics, we might go even deeper and maybe start looking inside electrons too!

It is very important to be able to see this fundamental difference between these three branches of physics.

Before you even begin, it is very important to ask this question—why do we study electricity and magnetism together? Why not study them separately? It is because they cannot exist in isolation! Wherever there is electricity, there will be magnetism, and vice versa. It can be argued that

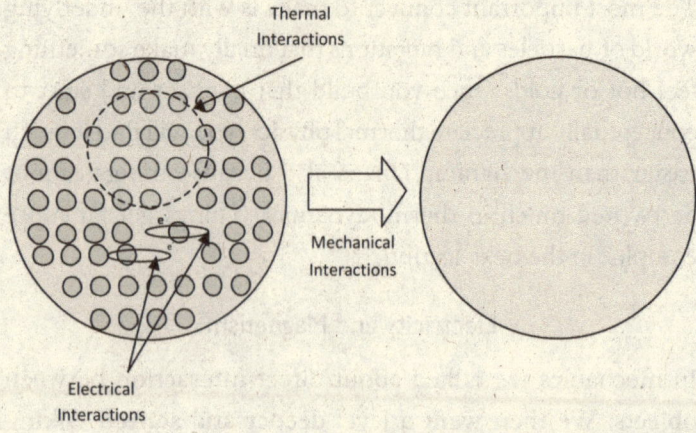

Thermal Interactions

Mechanical Interactions

Electrical Interactions

there is no magnetism when charges are stationary. But we all know that there is no such thing as stationary in physics. It all depends on the frame of reference. Hence you can simplify problems by looking at them through a frame that makes charges stationary; and then they become problems in electrostatics. As soon as charges begin to move, there is magnetism.

52. Coulomb's Law

All problems related to Coulomb's law are actually problems in mechanics and geometry masquerading as problems in electrostatics. Using Coulomb's law you should quickly find out the electrostatic forces and then solve the complete problem as for a mechanics problem, usually revolving around equilibrium. The two most important determinants of electrostatic forces are the signs of charges and the distances between them. So, first you must remember that likes repel and unlike charges attract each other. Simple though it sounds, it is very easy to mess this up under pressure. Also do a thorough recap of basic geometrical laws. Examiners love placing charges on triangles, squares and circles. So to calculate distance between charges you will have to apply geometry and trigonometry laws.

The last and most important point is that of *net* force. Before you actually start applying Coulomb's law to calculate the forces, it is important to use symmetry and cancel out as many forces as you can. This is easily achieved by drawing electrostatic force vectors on each charged particle. Once all the possible forces have been cancelled out along each dimension, you are left to calculate just the net force by applying the equations. Split each force into its horizontal and vertical component and solve the two directions separately in the problem, applying equilibrium independently along the two directions.

53. Fields

Fields are like astrological charts of space. They tell you beforehand what would happen if an object was placed at any point in that space. For example, we all know that objects fall down towards the earth. So, the field of earth's gravity would be arrows pointing towards the centre of the earth. These arrows help explain what would happen *if* an object was placed anywhere around the earth. Similarly, electric and magnetic fields tell you in advance what would happen if another electric charge was placed in a given space.

Calculating fields at a given point due to a charge distribution can be one of the most challenging problems in JEE if you haven't learnt the tricks of the trade. The most important component of any field problem is the identification of the infinitesimal charge and the integration along the entire uniformly charged body. A bit about coordinate conventions here—dx, dy and dz are used for infinitesimal distances along the axes in Cartesian coordinates, dr is used for radial distances while ds is used for curvature distances in spherical coordinates. If you stick to these conventions you will not get confused. You will usually be given the charge density of the object as either λ for linear density or σ for surface density. The key point again is to find symmetry in the problem. Divide the entire space into symmetrical sections around the point at which field is to be calculated. Pick an infinitesimal charge in each symmetrical segment and then calculate the *net* field on the point along each axis. Once whatever could be cancelled has been cancelled out, you'll be left with one net field along each axis. You can then integrate the field along the entire length of the charge. Practice is of prime importance here and you should solve as many different configurations of charges as possible.

Gauss's law also comes in very handy when solving field problems as long as you know where and how to apply it. The key is the ability to define a Gaussian surface. Two things to remember are that 1) a Gaussian surface is closed and 2) a Gaussian surface is chosen by you. The latter part is important and your choice should again be based on the symmetry of the problem.

54. Capacitance and Circuits

Fields are force per unit charge, while potential is energy per unit charge. Capacitors store energy due to the potential difference across their terminals. Then what is the difference between a battery and a capacitor? The difference is that in capacitors charge is conserved whereas in a battery the potential stays constant. A capacitor has no internal way of maintaining potential across itself; you always have to externally drive this potential. In a battery the electrochemical reactions within the battery always maintain this potential.

Solving circuits fast is a vital skill as the JEE paper always has a question involving circuits. The beauty and challenge lies in the fact that so many things can be clubbed together and hence tested simultaneously in circuit problems. The key tools in your kitty for these problems are as follows:

- Equations relating to potential and current or charge across elements. There are formulae for resistors, capacitors, inductors and even batteries (EMF = constant is also a formula).
- Equivalence rules for configuration of elements in series or parallel.

- Junction and loop rules relating to current across multi-loop circuits.

Using all of the above you should first solve for current in the various arms of a circuit. Once you have the current, you should then calculate potential at various points in the circuit. At times it may even be required to calculate charge, which is then nothing but current integrated over time.

55. Understanding Magnetism

Magnetism is borne of moving charges. All problems in magnetism require the ability to think in three dimensions as magnetic lines of force are always in a plane perpendicular to the direction of the movement of the charges. The right-hand-curl rule comes in handy to find the direction of these magnetic lines. You should always first establish the direction of the fields before attempting to apply any formulae. Also remember that the curl rule is for the right hand. Most students make the huge mistake of applying the left hand as they are usually writing with their right hands. Remember this, if you are a right-handed person, you will always have to put your pen down before applying the right-hand-curl rule. As long as you are crystal clear on vector concepts, especially cross products, have the basic ability to visualize things in three dimensions and can do simple integrations along linear paths, solving magnetism-related problems using the various laws like Biot–Savart and Ampere should not be very difficult.

While magnetism is caused by moving charges, or currents,

currents are induced by changing magnetic fields. The word 'changing' is very important here. Usually the best way to change magnetic fields passing through loops is to move the loop itself through a magnetic field. But remember that if the magnetic field is uniform, even moving a loop through it doesn't change the field through the loop when it is completely inside the magnetic field. It is only when it is entering or leaving the magnetic field that the field through it changes. So, the vital thing to remember is to always focus on the loop and see the magnetic field passing through the loop.

When solving circuits involving inductors, nothing new is needed. The same way of solving circuits applies. The only new things are the inductors and the rule connecting the potential across an inductor to the current flowing through it. Just make sure you never confuse the direction of current and the signs of potential differences and EMFs. This comes only by practice. So solve as many problems of RC, LR and RLC circuits as you can.

56. Lenses and Mirrors

In a system of lenses and mirrors, one should have the ability to visualize the impact of each lens and mirror separately as well as in combination with others. So, if a convex lens and a concave lens are kept next to each other, you should have a clear picture in your head as to where the image would be if either of these lenses were there all by themselves and then where the image would be when they were placed together.

One cannot hope to solve these systems without drawing them out on paper. Your ability to be able to draw parallel and perpendicular lines and draw lines at an angle quickly, without the need of a protractor, is going to be very important in solving these problems.

Images are formed by intersecting rays of light and virtual images are formed by virtual intersections. What are virtual intersections? These are intersections that would have happened if physical space did not prevent light rays from travelling. For example, in a plane mirror, light rays emerging from an object kept in front of it bounce off the surface and then diverge in the reverse direction. Assuming that space exists behind the mirror, the diverging rays would appear to be coming from a point source behind the mirror. This is a virtual image. A virtual image is created by your mind which believes everything to be simple and does not account for the presence of lenses and mirrors that are twisting the direction of rays of light. Our eyes always believe that light rays are travelling in straight lines and hence see things with that assumption. They cannot figure out that the straight rays of light that are reaching our eyes have bounced and bent many times through lenses and mirrors before they reach our eyes.

57. Electromagnetic Waves

There is a reason optics is placed after mechanics, waves, electricity and magnetism in the physics syllabus. Light is nothing but a transverse electromagnetic radiation at a special frequency to which human eyes are most sensitive. Whatever applies to light applies to any electromagnetic radiation. Electromagnetic radiations are nature's unique way of making energy travel without a medium. In an electromagnetic radiation, the electricity keeps the magnetism going and the magnetism keeps the electricity going. Both these fields push each other and the energy just travels forward. Beautiful! The key point to remember is that these oscillating electric and magnetic fields in an electromagnetic radiation are at right angles to each other. Also, the plane in which the electric field lies is the reference plane for the radiation and this plane can either stay fixed as the radiation travels forward or may keep changing in a predetermined manner. This is called polarization and materials that can change the natural state of polarization of radiation are called polarizers.

Interference happens when two different waves or electromagnetic radiations occupy a common space. In the case of mechanical waves, each wave exerts an individual force on the particles of the medium and the net force on the particles determines the final effect of this interference. In the case of electromagnetic radiations, there are no particles but there are fields. The resultant field due to these overlapping fields is what defines the net result of this interference. Depending on whether the fields are in the same direction and reinforce each other or are in opposite directions and cancel each other, the interference can be constructive or destructive. As long as you understand the true nature of electromagnetic radiation, conceptual problems related to interference and polarization are easy to address.

58. Modern Physics

You will have heard about the Higgs boson and the massive experiments that have been set up to discover it. The Higgs boson is most probably the last missing link in the theory of everything that will explain our entire universe perfectly, right from the moment the universe was created to the point when it will be destroyed. In fact, many claim this new physics will connect science to religion in ways we have not yet imagined. So, what is fondly called 'modern' physics is actually becoming the real physics of the twenty-first century, and very soon, maybe in just a few years, I think modern physics will be what is called physics and the everything else will become 'classical' or 'old' physics. Modern physics is very important for us to understand, more as a topic of current affairs and general knowledge than as a JEE subject.

Finally, modern physics and general physics are both equally necessary for the serious JEE contender. Students need modern physics to have the foundations to get into advanced topics in college. General physics prevents you from becoming too theoretical and ignoring some of the most wonderful experiments that lay the foundations of physics itself. Thus, each section of the syllabus has a reason to exist and an awareness of that reason will set the course for your preparation.

The most important thing to remember about modern physics is that the topic is vast and very complicated. So, extra care is taken to keep it simple and direct for JEE purposes. Hence, from the JEE perspective this topic will consist of mostly direct questions around the basic concepts and formulae. So make sure you score full marks in this section. All you need to do is go point by point according to the syllabus, making crisp notes on the key concepts and formulae, and revise it all thoroughly before the exam.

Physics in Summary

Across mechanics, heat, electricity, magnetism, optics and modern physics, a whole new world is opened up for you in JEE. The biggest effort you will have to make is to modify and expand the boundaries of your intuition. There are things from your schooldays that you have to unlearn or relearn in a completely different way. So, be prepared to challenge those long-held intuitive concepts. A lot of students question why they were taught incomplete or 'wrong' things in lower classes if this is what the science really is. Well, trust me, whatever physics you are learning for JEE will also have to be unlearnt and relearnt when you are in IIT. However, as goes the famous Morpheus quote from *The Matrix Reloaded* (2003): 'There are some things in this world, Captain Niobe, that will never change . . . Some things do change.' While the way things are taught keeps changing due to the increasing maturity of the minds they are taught to, the fundamental laws of nature that physics teaches us remain essentially the same.

CHEMISTRY

Going by experience, I think chemistry proves to be the holy grail for a lot of IIT aspirants. This is not really surprising as chemistry is very different from mathematics and physics. Chemistry has more to it than just numbers and mathematical equations. It's got different colours and shapes to consider and too many particles migrating from one orbit to another to be entirely straightforward. Chemistry has an element of mystery to it and as such its preparation requires a completely different approach as compared to the other two subjects. Chemistry is about creation. It's the art (and science) of substances reacting together and forming a completely different compound. I say art because there is very little logical prediction that one can do. Remember, first came the reactions and then came the explanation for those reactions. In short, chemistry is the fun element in the otherwise dry world of JEE and requires you to be a little creative, imaginative and open-minded.

Since chemistry controls one-third of the JEE marks, you can't ignore it. I have often seen students ignore the subject because they think they just cannot memorize the colours of compounds, the reaction mechanisms, the compound properties, etc. What they forget is that chemistry is the rank decider and often the difference between selection and a good rank. Most topics in chemistry are straightforward. While physical chemistry is about application, inorganic questions are more direct in nature and do not need much calculation. You need to plan how to approach each of the three sub-parts (physical, inorganic, organic) as a one-size-fits-all approach will not work. If you do not pay enough attention to chemistry you can kiss a good JEE rank goodbye.

JEE chemistry has three sub-parts: physical chemistry, inorganic chemistry and organic chemistry. Physical chemistry is largely number-driven and very similar in concept to physics while the other two sub-parts—inorganic chemistry and organic chemistry—are more about the properties of various inorganic and organic compounds, the various reaction mechanisms, etc. The latter two are 'softer' and do not involve any kind of hard skills such as number-crunching. Inorganic and organic chemistry involve more memorizing than physical chemistry, so I like to treat them as two different sets of topics and not three. In the following pages, however, I'll discuss how to prepare for the three topics separately.

59. Treat Chemistry on Par

The moment you enter class eleven, you will find everyone advising you to just focus on the concepts and not worry too much about solving too many questions. This is exactly what I have also advised in the previous pages, but there is a catch here. I have often found that students get so engrossed in learning the concepts in physics and mathematics that they find learning the reaction mechanisms in chemistry boring. They want to know the concept behind the reaction and lose heart when they find that the mechanisms changes from reaction to reaction and that there are a great many exceptions. They devote too much time to physics and mathematics and treat chemistry (especially inorganic and organic) as the stepchild in their JEE preparation.

Preparing for chemistry (inorganic and organic) requires you to devote sufficient time to the topics to let them sink in. You will not be able to grasp it all in one sitting and then go on to solve any problem related to it. You will have to internalize a few of the mechanisms and a lot of exceptions. More than anything else, you'll require a change of mindset when it comes to preparing JEE chemistry. You have to understand that here is a subject that is going to make your rank. All you have to do is to keep on reading and rereading it so that the concepts become part of your long-term memory. You just can't leave the subject for the last few days. After all, it's one-third of the total JEE marks and you will have to treat it on par with physics and mathematics.

It's a fair game. Chemistry is the fairest game of all—if you devote time to it, you will get rewarded fair and square. You can spend a few hundred hours doing integration problems, but JEE might still stump you with one that you struggle to crack. Not so with chemistry—if there is a particular section to which you have devoted enough attention, you will be duly rewarded. Another important fact about JEE chemistry is that it is a real timesaver in objective questions.

Most chemistry questions are rather direct and either you know the answer or you don't. There isn't much figuring out that you need to do. So, more often than not you will be able to wrap up chemistry in less than one-third the total time and save some precious minutes for tricky questions in mathematics or physics.

Actually, preparing for JEE chemistry is easier than it seems. Chemistry is essentially a game of practice: the more you do it, the better you get at it.

Inorganic Chemistry

Get ready to be lost in a world of reactions. Inorganic chemistry is the colourful part of the JEE syllabus with compound colours covering the entire spectrum of VIBGYOR. This branch of chemistry is about the properties of various chemical compounds and elements. It requires you to learn by heart various reactions, colours, names and the chemical formulae of the compounds formed as a result of these reactions. It is one of the best scoring areas in the entire JEE syllabus. It is generally binary in its nature, that is, if you know the reaction and the properties of the compounds formed, you can solve a question in just three seconds, and if you don't know the reaction then you're just shooting the dark and it's better not to guess the right answer. That is why inorganic chemistry plays a huge role in deciding the overall rank. A solid grounding in inorganic chemistry is generally the difference between a great rank and a good rank.

60. Start Preparing in Class Eleven

Inorganic chemistry is one of those subjects in which the more time you spend, the better you get. It involves a fair amount of learning and cramming of reactions, elements, compounds and their properties. So, it is best to start early, in class eleven itself. I'm not suggesting that you start learning inorganic from day one. Ideally, you should start reading it when you get a little comfortable with the JEE preparation and settle down into a routine where you can take out some time, let's say two to three days a week or some hours over the weekend to devote a few hours to the subject.

I personally feel it is a mistake to not start inorganic chemistry before class twelve. What students don't realize is that in class twelve they will have to consolidate and revise the syllabus of the entire two years, and leaving a subject as big as inorganic chemistry to a later stage will only add to their anxiety. They will not be able to do justice to the subject. *The trick of the game is to start early so that you can revise the syllabus multiple times before class twelve.* Inorganic chemistry is all about practice and getting familiar with the reactions and the colours of the compounds involved in these reactions. The more you read it, the deeper it gets engraved in your memory. In the following pages, I will tell you how to prepare a special notebook for this subject. Once you have created that notebook, all you have to do is to read it whenever you find time. Read it on your way to school, read it before going to bed.

61. The Colour-Coded Notebook

A picture is worth a thousand words. This is because the human mind has the ability to retain information in the form of pictures and graphics. All of us can easily remember scenes from our favourite movies and recall some of the posters or paintings that we liked. This ability can be leveraged to learn and remember new signs, languages and, yes, inorganic chemistry. Inorganic chemistry in its basic form is a kind of language. It has its own alphabets (elements and compounds) and rules (reaction mechanisms). Thus, one of the best ways to learn inorganic chemistry reactions is to create a colour-coded image for each reaction.

How do you create an image from a reaction? Well, it's simple. All you need is a sketch-pen set and you are ready. Write down the reaction in your notebook. Now create a small box around every compound/element of the reaction and fill it with the colour of that particular compound/element. So, a sample equation will look something like this:

$$\boxed{Cu} \quad + \quad \boxed{H_2SO_4} \quad = \quad \boxed{CuSO_4}$$

☐ Copper   ☐ White   ■ Blue

Now, this may look like a tedious job and some of you may actually think that it's not worth the effort. Please feel free to agree or disagree with this method of learning about the colours and properties of inorganic chemical reactions.

I found it particularly useful because it made sure that I created interesting memories like searching for the right colour, colouring the notebook, creating my symbols indicating the thermal nature of the reaction, etc.* This approach made memorizing chemical reactions more fun than conventional methods.

Keep a set of sketch pens handy and whenever you come across a new reaction, just write it in this notebook and colour-code it. If you think you won't find time to do it during the lectures, you can create a separate notebook where you rewrite the reactions you have learnt in class and use it for revision. You can create your own effects for exothermic reactions (flames), precipitations reactions (flakes), etc. This notebook will become your guide to success in inorganic chemistry. You should keep on writing new reactions in this notebook for the next two years (make sure it's a good-quality notebook that can last that long). This is the notebook that you'll have to read over and over again so that you can relate a reaction to its image and easily recall the colours and other properties of the chemicals involved. While making this notebook takes considerable time, towards the end of two years you'll realize that it was well worth the effort. So, whip out those sketch pens and start adding some colour to those chemical reactions.

62. Use the Laboratory

Since the convergence of the JEE and NCERT syllabi over the years, the NCERT textbook has actually become the prescribed

* Paras.

reading for JEE chemistry. However, what is often seen is that students preparing for JEE do not pay enough attention to the school curriculum. The focus shifts to the coaching classes and school takes a back seat. I have noticed students miss classes in school to attend coaching sessions. While missing a few classes will be detrimental to your overall performance, what will really harm you is missing the various practical laboratory sessions. Practical labs are a great way to learn and have fun at the same time. Labs help you cement the classroom learning into your long-term memory by giving you a chance to actually do the reactions and see for yourself how various elements react and form compounds with each other. You'll never forget a reaction you performed yourself. The moment someone asks you about a reaction you have performed, your mind will go back to that moment, the colour of the compounds/elements involved, the colour of the reaction precipitate, etc. There is no better way to learn inorganic chemistry than by actually conducting the experiments in a laboratory.

There are a few coaching institutes that specialize in chemistry. I've heard about classes where the teacher actually performed each and every reaction as he wrote them on the board. He showed the entire class how the various reactants react and how new compounds are formed. If you find a centre which gives you live demonstrations of the reactions, I'd say go for it. Alternatively, you can try and find a lab in your town which can help you perform these reactions, perhaps during your summer breaks.

If you think that attending a chemistry lab for a few hours a week is a sub-optimal utilization of time, you couldn't be more wrong. Treat this lab time as a fun way of de-stressing and learning at the same time. So, go to a lab and precipitate that calcium, make that blue vitriol (Cu_2SO_4) and see the real-world application of the reactions that you may have read. All the fumes of the chemicals, the bursting of test tubes, the change of colours will come back to you in the hour of need during the JEE examination.

63. Reaction Cards

Remember the WWE trading cards? The Rock, Stone Cold, The Undertaker? Remember how you knew by heart a lot of WWE details (height, weight, biceps, fights won, etc.) from these cards? You always knew which card to play when and what information to ask for so you could stump your rival. It was the competitive spirit and a desire to win the game that made sure you had memorized all the information from a lot of these cards. Now is the time to channel that energy and motivation into learning inorganic chemistry.

Confused? Well, you will still play with the trading cards but the characters will change. The overgrown WWE characters will now be replaced by acids and bases (yes, life is sometimes cruel). You'll be competing with your friends to tell the colours and chemical formulae of the reactants and the by-products involved in a reaction.

You must now be wondering how you can possibly make a

card for every reaction. This is where teamwork will come to the rescue. Team up with a few friends and divide the making of the reaction cards amongst yourselves. While these cards may be available in the market, I suggest that you make them yourself. The information in inorganic chemistry cards is often incorrect in non-reliable sources and it is better to stick to good sources of information while making your own cards. Make sure you make them out of paper or cardboard which will last you the two years. (Or maybe it's better to prepare these cards again. Practise!) While creating these cards, make sure the following details are present: the chemicals involved, their colours, precipitation, chemical formulae, scientific as well as household names, the thermal (endothermic, exothermic) nature of the reaction, etc. You must write all the details of the reaction on one side of the card and just the reaction (only chemical names and no formulae) on the other side.

Once you have prepared these cards, you must challenge each other to tell as many details as possible about a particular

Copper + Sulphuric Acid	$Cu + H_2SO_4 \rightarrow CuSO_4.5H_2O$ Colour: **Blue** Household Name: **Blue Vitriol** Scientific Name: **Copper Sulphate Pentahydrate** $CuSO_4.5H_2O \xrightarrow{Heat} CuSO_4.H_2O \xrightarrow{Heat} CuSO_4$ (White)
Front	Back

reaction. Show the names of the chemicals involved (say, copper and sulphuric acid) written on the front of the card and ask your friend for the complete reaction, the colours and other properties, the different variants of products formed ($5H_2O$, $1H_2O$), and so on.

64. All You Need Is a Push

I was never a big fan of inorganic chemistry.* In fact, I was afraid of it. Nothing scared me more than the thought of colouring my notebook and remembering the random equations. For me, the equations never made any sense, though I would try to reason why this compound was blue and that one green. Luckily, I had a teacher who knew that I was not really excited about the subject. He started pushing me. Every morning as I entered the class, I would be asked to complete a reaction and state the colours of the compounds involved. If I failed I was made to stand for the next two hours and had to attend the lecture from one corner of the classroom. And God forbid I forgot the sketch pens! That meant going back home or buying a new set. In the beginning it was irritating and I wanted to stop attending his classes, but after a week of standing in the cold, I said to myself, 'Kitna hi mushkil hoga yaar! Bahut hua!' (Enough is enough! How difficult can it be!) No one else was going to have early-morning fun at my expense and so I started

* Paras.

reading the equations that were taught the previous day. Yes, I answered the questions about the equations on the board the next day, but then I was asked equations from the previous week and there I was, standing in a corner all over again. However, I had bitten the bullet and now I knew it was not really difficult to get those equations into my head.

What I'm trying to say is that sometimes it's nice to have someone around who pushes you. If you are not lucky enough to find such a teacher, create a group of friends where you can all push each other. Decide on five or ten new reactions that each one of you has to learn every day and you can quiz each other on any of those reactions at any time the next day. You can place a bet when someone is not able to answer. Remember, these five or ten reactions keep adding up, and whatever was supposed to be learnt since the beginning of the exercise is fair game.

65. Mnemonics

Mnemonics are a great memory aid. A mnemonic translates information in a way that helps the human brain retain it longer. These are great tools to memorize new symbols, languages, etc. One of the first mnemonics that we all learnt was to remember the days in a month by using the knuckles on our fists. Each knuckle meant the month had 31 days and each trough meant 30 (28/29 in case of February). Such tools help in transferring information into the long-term memory and also create strong linkages so that you can recall the requisite information any time you need. Remembering information is more about linkages than about storage space. The mind is capable of storing very large amounts of information, but if the information is not used for a long time, the linkage to the storage becomes weak and we are not able to recall the information we need. Mnemonics help in creating strong linkages by associating information with a song or a tune or an action. When the brain recalls the tune or action, it invokes the storage to provide the necessary data. Other such tools are making short poems, short stories or memorable phrases out of the information you wish to retain.

The reason mnemonics works well for inorganic chemistry is because the subject has its own language with its own symbols and rules. There is, for example, very little logical sense about why copper is called copper. It is just called copper. Nor is why sodium called sodium is something that has a great deal of logic or reasoning behind it.

Create small mnemonics for various reactions that you find hard to remember. Build a small story about how copper was walking down the road on a hot, rainy morning and fell into a pit of boiling liquid that turned out to be sulphuric acid. Copper struggled and gasped for breath but sank deep. Finally copper re-emerged but was all blue and had five balloons of water all around itself.

Another useful mnemonic for the periodic table is as follows:

h(a) he le be, b(a)K N(a) o funny, na mug alsi PasCl Arkca.
Shakti Vikarman feCo Niku jan

66. Recorded Tapes

How many times have you found yourself humming a song, which you had heard a long time ago, the moment your radio started playing it? Suddenly the lyrics come back to you and you can sing along in almost perfect sync with the radio. Very often you can clearly make out when someone sings the wrong lyrics. You may not know the correct lyrics yourself but you can easily point out the wrong ones. Use this ability of your mind—to recollect information the moment it hears something familiar—to memorize inorganic chemistry reactions.

I found it difficult to carry my colour-coded inorganic chemistry notebook with me (especially after it had gone through over one and a half years of abuse).[*] So I decided to record the reactions on audio tapes and listen to them using my walkman (yes, I come from the era of walkmans!). Use a recording instrument (all you need is a microphone and recording software) and record the reactions in your own voice. Recording the reactions in your own voice will help you immediately connect with the notebook and visualize the colours when you hear them. You will see for yourself how easily you'll be able to recollect the relevant page and

[*] Paras.

the coloured boxes of the notebook the moment you hear a reaction.

You could use an iPod or an MP3 player and listen to these recordings whenever you get time—while waiting at a bus stop, travelling in the Metro, and so on. Ideally, you should switch between music and chemistry so that it does not become monotonous. When you listen to a reaction, say it inside your head so that you can imprint it on your long-term memory. In the final exam, while solving a problem, say the reaction inside your head and the exact reaction will come back to you and it will all be music to your ears.

67. Stare at the Wall

I don't know about you but some of the most profound thoughts come to me inside the restroom. If you are one of those who like to read their newspaper in the comfort of their restrooms, then this tip is especially for you. Somehow, the mind works at its best during those ten or fifteen minutes, and one is able to soak in more information than it can at other times. This is the perfect time to download chemical reactions into your system. Just write a few reactions on two sheets of paper (in a large font and with sketch pens) and paste them on the wall in front of your toilet seat. Give them a read when you're going through your morning routine. Replace the sheets once every ten days or move them to a corner and paste new sheets with new reactions in the centre.

Note: you can choose some other wall and paste these sheets there. The important thing is to have some time dedicated to reading these reactions for a few minutes every day. If you think pasting the reactions on the ceiling works for you then go ahead and paste them there.

Physical Chemistry

Physical chemistry is by far the most logical and number-driven field of chemistry. It is very similar to physics and mathematics because it follows certain well-defined rules and equations. It has only a few concepts and does not require you to remember any reaction mechanisms or properties of various chemical compounds. Therefore, it is the easiest among the three parts of JEE chemistry. It is also a scoring subject for most successful JEE candidates. There are very few concepts and very standard problems. Rarely will you find a problem in physical chemistry that requires imagination and improvisation. Generally, it will not pose a huge challenge.

Preparing for physical chemistry is actually really easy. There are no major tips or special techniques to crack this topic. It requires you to understand and remember the formulae and know how to apply them. While inorganic and organic chemistry are tricky and may require you to read different concepts from different books, physical chemistry is rather simple and it would be best to stick to the standard books.

68. Skip the Calculator

Physical chemistry requires you to be fast and accurate with numbers. You'll be dealing with numbers up to three decimal places. I have often found that many students take the easy way out and pick up the calculator to solve the problems. Actually, most physical chemistry problems can easily be solved with just a calculator (no pen or paper required). However, you will not get the luxury of a calculator in the final exam. You'll have to manually do the calculations and you need to be fast with them. Make it a habit to do the numbers manually and use a calculator only when you're doing quick revisions.

69. Complete the Topic in Class Eleven

The physical chemistry syllabus for JEE is not huge and can be easily covered in class eleven. It is best to complete the entire portion or most of it in the first year of your JEE preparation. But you must realize that if you're comfortable with the pace of the subject in your school or coaching class, there is no reason to force yourself to finish the topic in class eleven. The underlying point here is that wrapping up physical chemistry should not come at the expense of other subjects. So, follow an approach that you are comfortable with and do not push if you feel you're not able to devote sufficient time to other subjects in your hurry to finish this one.

Organic Chemistry

Organic chemistry just like inorganic—they are both primarily about reactions and reaction mechanisms. Organic is slightly easier than inorganic (in my opinion) as there are no colours to remember. But just like we saw in inorganic chemistry, first came the complex organic compounds and then came the explanation for the reactions resulting in these compounds. So, you will have to go through the same process of understanding and learning the reaction mechanisms and applying them over and over again.

While the scope of inorganic chemistry is vast, the JEE syllabus has a limited number of concepts in its organic chemistry section. So your life will be much easier while preparing for organic as compared to inorganic.

70. Rewrite the Entire Notebook

One of my organic chemistry professors had a unique way of teaching the subject.* He would explain the reaction mechanisms, show a few examples and then ask us to do a few practice problems. The next day's lecture would begin with ten reaction questions written on the board and anyone could be called upon to solve them. We were expected to solve them correctly in the very little time that he would give us. The lecture would not begin till all the ten reactions had been

* Paras.

solved (this sometimes meant that almost the entire class had to make a trip to the whiteboard). For those who could not solve the reaction, the rule was simple. By the next class they had to turn in a notebook covering all the reaction mechanisms taught till that point. This meant that unlucky souls like me had to rewrite every reaction at least four times in the course of the year. Now, you may call this method extreme and actually label me stupid for rewriting the entire notebook four times, but I definitely benefited from this process. It made sure that I was able to iron out my weaknesses by this rather crude and repetitive method, because left to my own devices I would not have given it as much attention.

Another important point to note here is that even though it meant a lot of hard work, I did not back out of the effort. I could have conveniently taken the easier route, like some of my classmates, by skipping the next few classes, but that would have meant giving up without trying. You have to understand that it is important for you to learn something that you may not find interesting, if only because you want to excel in JEE. You will have to fight that urge to give up and focus on other more interesting topics, because by doing so you'll be cheating yourself and no one else. Stay true to the goal that you have set for yourself and keep progressing towards it, one step at a time.

Chemistry in Summary

Chemistry is all about practice. Inorganic and organic chemistry require you to practise the reaction mechanisms, while physical chemistry requires you to practise calculation so you can quickly solve problems. I had a lot of problems with inorganic and organic in the beginning but reminded myself of the importance of clearing the cut-off in the final exam.[*] I laboured through it in the initial months but in the end I was comfortable with the concepts while writing the JEE chemistry exam. The final piece of advice for chemistry is: Stay with it and your problems will sort themselves out.

MATHEMATICS

Be prepared for a lot of brevity here. There is not much that can be taught in mathematics. It is mostly about figuring things out by doing them yourself. Pedagogically speaking, there is a list of formulae, theorems, axioms, lemmas, etc. A teacher or a book can explain them to you, but applying them to problems and figuring out which one would be the most useful in which situation is a practitioner's art and prerogative. Mathematics is not exactly teachable; it has to be learnt. Probably that is why students are so scared of this subject. I will share with you the tips that worked for me.

71. Practice

There is no such thing as a book on mathematics, only workbooks. Mathematics is learnt by using pen and paper, never by reading. Every moment in mathematics spent reading

[*] Paras.

is a waste of time. Notes will not help you here so don't bother with them. Each and every rule, theorem, principle and formula has to be learnt by applying it in problems. Practice also increases speed, which is of key importance in JEE. There is no such thing as an easy problem in JEE. The easiest of problems can create 'differentials' in ranks by way of the time each individual takes in arriving at the answer to that easy problem. So, keep practising maths because 1) it is the only way to learn maths, 2) it reduces your chances of making silly mistakes and 3) it increases the speed at which you solve problems. There is a simple golden rule for mathematics—*If you don't use it, you'll lose it.*

72. Approach

Mathematics can get quite convoluted and scary. Problems can get very esoteric and abstract. Proofs can run into many pages. You have to stay away from such scary material. JEE is an entrance examination for engineering. Engineers build things that make life easy for mankind, so they only need to know as much maths as can help them build things. They need to reach answers quickly. So be very cautious when attempting overwhelmingly difficult problems in mathematics. Maybe you don't need to go that deep!

If you're preparing for the mathematics Olympiad or want to be an ace mathematician, go deep by all means. Maths does not disappoint deep-sea divers. But success in the subject is to be able to come back to the surface with something new inside your brain rather than just sinking deeper and deeper and then drowning. Stay away from concepts that you don't need to know for JEE. Maths is far too vast.

73. Graphical Representation

The ability to work out problems graphically is very important to succeed in JEE maths, so you should work very hard on this skill. Every time you see algebraic equations, you should immediately create their graphical counterparts. Linear equations, simultaneous equations, quadratic equations and inequalities all can be, and should be, visualized and solved graphically. Like everything in mathematics, this ability is developed only by practice.

74. Substitutions

Being able to substitute is another key skill in mathematics. Substitutions have the power to reduce complex problems into simple and familiar representations. This is again developed only by practising different kinds of problems. Here is a nice way to think about substitutions. Imagine a staircase where the size of the stairs keeps decreasing. So initially the stairs are big, then they get smaller and smaller, until the way becomes almost a keyhole. If Russian nesting dolls were to climb these stairs, they would first all sit inside the biggest doll, then, as the stairs got narrower, one after the other the smaller ones would come out, until, finally, the smallest (and cutest) among them would be able to squeeze through the last few stairs.

In the same way, mathematical problems can be seen as a narrowing staircase. You first reduce the bigger parts by clubbing together expressions into one variable. Then, as you try to get to the final solution, you expand the variables like you open up Russian dolls.

A simple example could be trying to differentiate the expression $x^4 + 2x^2e^x + e^{2x}$. One way of doing it is going term by term and applying the product rule on term 2. Another way is to have the eye quickly see that this is nothing but $(x^2 + e^x)^2$ and hence you can solve this by simply substituting $y = x^2 + e^x$. So y is now the bigger Russian doll, you walk the bigger step by reducing y^2 to $2y$ and then open up the bigger doll y to extract the inner dolls $x^2 + e^x$.

75. Formulae Lists and Keys

For some people, mathematics is nothing but a jungle of formulae. That doesn't mean you just stop and stare at the jungle and don't enter it. You have to enter it. Only once you cut through the dense undergrowth of creepy formulae will you reach the heart of the forest where there are beautiful fountains and bright sunshine. In short, formulae are a necessary evil and once you get through them you see the real beauty of mathematics.

How do you get through this forest? The easiest and proven way of doing this is to have formulae lists and keys. Not borrowed or printed ones, please; use only handwritten ones that you make yourself. Only you know which formulae you need to remember. Someone else's list may not have something that you always forget and have something that you remember by heart.

76. The Vedic Age Was 4000 Years Ago

Vedic mathematics is very close to our hearts. It is the wisdom of ancient India passed down over generations and has survived 4000 years of changing times, continuing to enthral academicians and historians around the world. As someone with a taste for ancient history I have immense respect for Vedic mathematics and I would encourage every engineer, nay every student, to read and know more about it.[*] And I would say the same about *Arthashastra*, *Malavikagnimitram*, *Abhigyan Shakuntalam*, the *Principia Mathematica* and the *Indica*. But does that mean any of these are remotely relevant for JEE? *NO!*

[*] Vivek.

There are shortcuts and methods in Vedic maths to do simple things like multiplication and division. Rest assured the JEE examiner will never give you problems where you need to multiply nine-digit numbers or divide fifteen-digit numbers by eleven-digit numbers. If you are preparing for the Olympiad, indulge yourself by all means. But Vedic maths is not part of the JEE syllabus (say it again). Repeat this to anyone who suggests that you buy pop booklets on Vedic maths or join the evening classes of a Vedic maths guru.

77. Complex Numbers

It is a little difficult to appreciate what complex numbers are and why we need them. In many branches of engineering, complex numbers make life very simple when solving problems. The kinds of problems students solve in school do not need complex numbers, but the kind of problems they will be solving in an engineering college will require them. As students, you must humbly accept that knowing how to use complex numbers is going to be very important in your engineering career and that is why it is part of the JEE syllabus.

Complex numbers have three different representations—the basic, the geometric and the Euler representations. You must master the art of converting each of these forms into the others, knowing which representation works best in what kinds of problems, and also acquire the ability to do all the complex-number operations like addition, subtraction, multiplication, division and roots in each format. This is where practice comes in handy because with practice you can quickly visualize the first few steps of the solution without actually having to spend time working it out. Hence, you can quickly evaluate the best approach to solving a problem by mentally trying out a few alternatives.

You should also understand the complete separation of the real and imaginary parts of a complex number. They are completely independent of each other and hence a simple complex-number equation is always two simultaneous equations—of the real and the imaginary parts.

Two things you must be able to do at lightning speed: one is to compute powers of i and –i, and the other is to know the trigonometric ratios for all angles in multiples of $15°$ ($n\pi/12$). The number i (also π and e) is one of the foundation concepts of JEE mathematics and you should understand and accept it early in your preparation. Although trigonometry comes much later in your syllabus, success in complex numbers depends a lot on your mastery over basic trigonometric laws and the values of the ratios of key angles.

78. Quadratic Equations

Quadratic equations have to first be reduced to the standard form $ax^2 + bx + c$ and then the rules governing the constants a, b and c have to be applied. This is the approach that always works. It is important to not get overwhelmed by the complexity of any equation. It is quite likely that a, b and c are made to be very complex, but the simple rules connecting them to the roots stay the same. Substitutions and graphical representations are both extremely important in solving quadratic equations. Also note that since the rules for real roots of quadratic equations are in the form of an inequality, a lot of interesting inequality problems are framed using quadratic equations.

79. Series and Progressions

In problems on series and progressions you have to be very careful about indices and their ranges. Mostly indices start from 0 and hence for n terms, they end at a value of $(n - 1)$. This is the source of many a careless mistake.

Another important skill to have is to be able to see which terms will remain and which will fall off as the series progresses. For example, if a series has a term $x^{-n} + e^{-nx}$, you should be able to immediately see that both these terms will fall off, or become zero, as the series progresses and goes to infinity. Also remember that the concept of greater and lesser becomes meaningless when we are dealing with infinity. While $5x > 2x$ when x is finite and positive, both become equal to infinity as x tends to infinity. It is difficult to digest in the beginning that unequal things all tend to either zero or infinity as a series progresses. It can be related to divinity, if you think of it that way. Rich or poor, smart or foolish, all go to either heaven or hell in the long term. So 3n or 4m or $x^{-n} + e^{-nx}$ all will go to either zero or infinity as n and m become larger and larger.

80. Permutations and Combinations

In this topic, getting used to the notation takes a while but once you have got used to it the problems tend to be relatively easy to solve. There are two kinds of challenges in this domain— problem formulation and expression reduction.

Problem formulation involves situations with dice, coloured balls, people sitting at a table, etc. This is so amenable to conjuring up new situations that falling into a standardized approach is the biggest risk. Rest assured the examiner will find an entirely new kind of problem to ask you and you have to be conceptually very strong rather than fall into the trap of memorizing standard problems. Again, practice is important but the trick is to use as many solved problems as possible. Attempt it on your own, then see the correct solution and try to find out where exactly you made a mistake or deviated from what the author has done. Correcting your approach bit by bit is very important.

For the expression-reduction problems, make sure you memorize as many shortcuts as possible. There are lots of derived results for permutation and combination terms. The more you remember, the faster you'll be able to reduce complex expressions.

81. Matrices

This is probably one of the easier topics at the JEE level. Matrices become extremely intricate at undergrad and degree levels and are used in almost every computational topic, but right now, enjoy the simplicity. As in all simple topics, the key is to take extreme care and not make silly mistakes. Multiplying two matrices is something you should practise as it is error-prone.

The only other thing to keep in mind is what the various kinds of matrices and their properties are. Any good book or coaching will do. There are also a lot of simple rules around matrices, like the multiplication of two triangular matrices is always a triangular matrix, the value of the determinant is the same when expanded by any row or any column, and so on. The more of these rules you remember, the faster you can solve your matrices problems. In fact, these rules come in very handy in advanced scientific and engineering subjects as well. For example, trying to invert a matrix is a little tough at times. You can compute its determinant in advance and if it is zero, you know upfront that it is not invertible. So, why waste time? Diagonal and identity matrices also have some beautiful properties. Hence, in matrix problems people usually rush to reduce matrices to diagonal or identity forms because they can then apply these rules of thumb and reach conclusions quickly.

82. Probability

You can be strong in probability only if you are strong in permutations and combinations, so make sure you perfect the latter before you start the former. The only really new concept in probability is conditional probability and Bayes' theorem. This is a topic that you have to understand and appreciate. Solving a large number of problems may not really help much if you don't spend time thinking about the conceptual underpinnings. Probability takes a lot of time to really sink in. You have to start using it in your day-to-day happenings and keep thinking in those terms all the time to ground yourself. For example, whenever you leave for school think about the probability of you reaching school on time. Yes, there is a way to find a probability for almost any event, so take any event and try to think through the probability of it happening. Another interesting example could be: What is the probability that you will sit next to a girl in class today (as opposed to a boy)? Developing a fun approach to probability is essential and comes naturally after some time.

83. Trigonometry

Trigonometry doesn't start with 'T'; it starts with 'π'. Understand pi and you have understood half of trigonometry. When someone asks you what pi is, please never say it is 22/7. Pi is the ratio of a circle's circumference to its diameter. No one can ever tell the exact value of pi. People have calculated it to a lot of decimal places but it just doesn't end. So take some time to understand what pi is. Also, you will now have to increasingly work with radians so the sooner you come out of the habit of using degrees, the better it is for you. Instead of an angle of $30°$, you should start saying an angle of $\pi/6$ radians. Once you are comfortable with pi and radians, it is time to start memorizing. Yes, mathematics does demand a good memory. Trigonometric ratios for all key angles have to be remembered; also to be remembered are complex formulae for the sums and differences of angles and the relationships among trigonometric ratios. These are best done using charts (see Tip #25).

It would be unfair at this point to not mention the classic text *Plane Trigonometry* by S.L. Loney. It is a thin book written by a nineteenth-century mathematician, but it is one of the most thorough texts on trigonometry till date. Follow that book and you will be amazed at the way it deals with the topics.

84. Analytical Geometry

This is where algebra officially meets geometry. If you had any illusions that you could handle equations without drawing curves, they will now be rudely shattered as you'll have to understand curves through equations. It is important here to ponder over something—what is really a curve and what is an equation? They are nothing but constraints or rules. Space is open and unconstrained. If there are no rules, anyone can go anywhere. But the universe has rules and so any interesting movement or structure in space will be following some rules. It is these rules that are written as equations and expressed as curves. Spend some time thinking about this—it will blow your mind. I feel this is one of the hardest sections in mathematics as your visualization and analytical skills are tested simultaneously. As for the specific topics, there is no major tip that I can give you apart from the usual one—practise!

85. Differential Calculus

Calculus is supposed to be the hottest topic when students pick up college-level mathematics. Before you even think of starting differential or integral calculus, you must ground yourself deeply in the concept of functions. The things that are most important to know about functions are the main types of functions and their main properties. The types of functions are polynomial, rational, exponential, logarithmic and trigonometric. One very important concept to understand is that of the number e. As already mentioned in the section on complex numbers (Tip #77), e, π and i are the foundation symbols/concepts of mathematics and must be respected and understood thoroughly. The properties of functions are whether they are even or odd, their domain, singularity, slope, discontinuity, inverse, etc.

Before you try to find the limit of functions or begin to differentiate them, first understand them and the various types and terms associated with them. It would be worthwhile to dedicate a week on just building your foundations in functions. These foundations are far more important than knowing how to differentiate functions.

Of course, once you are through with this you have to get to calculus. But wait, there is one more thing, and that is the concept of the infinitesimal and infinity. A lot of derivations and theorems in calculus, in fact probably the whole of calculus, rest on this one single concept; so without truly appreciating it, there is no moving forward. The infinitesimal is smaller than every possible real number you can think of and yet it is not zero. I thought of it like this: suppose there is a wall and you are standing at a certain distance from it. Each second you cover half the distance from the wall. When will you touch the wall? Beginners would say two seconds, but those who know the concepts of infinitesimal and infinity would say that you will never touch the wall! Because the 'half' is calculated from the remaining distance every time. So if you start at one foot, in one second you will be at half a foot, in two seconds at a quarter of a foot, and on and on like this. But the distance will never be zero. Ultimately, the distance would be smaller than the smallest number conceivable, just short of zero. This 'ultimately' is called infinity and this smallest distance is called the infinitesimal.

Substitutions and rules of differentiation of sum, product and quotient of two functions and rules for differentiating a function of a function are probably the only tools you will need to get through.

86. Integral Calculus

Finally we come to integration, which is always seen as the reverse of differentiation. That is where students go wrong. I would suggest that from the very beginning you look at integration as an area under a curve and differentiation as the slope of the curve. Most of the problems in JEE are best handled with this understanding rather than any other.

The methods of partial fractions and substitutions, like

almost all intricate topics in maths, need to be practised a lot. Before practice, looking at a lot of solved problems could be very helpful. While I have clearly mentioned the limited role of books and teachers in maths, they can add a lot of value in this case by walking you through various possible approaches to solving different problems. The more you see, the better equipped you will be to use them when solving problems.

One of the most important skills in integral calculus is the ability to pick functions within functions. It is like being able to read backwards and it is a skill that takes some practice to develop. There is a standard rule to pick functions and goes by the name of LIATE. So you pick L for logarithmic, then I for inverse trigonometric, A for algebraic, T for trigonometric and then E for exponential, in that order. This is like the BODMAS of integral calculus. It might be anathema to purists to learn a pattern by rote, but we are not purists, are we? We are players of the big JEE war and in war a few neat tricks up your sleeve always help.

87. Vectors

Vectors, like matrices, are an essential part of an engineer's and a scientist's toolkits. Improper or incomplete grounding in vectors might not cost you your JEE seat since the vector problems in JEE are simple and few and can usually be solved with a little practice. Later, though, it might cost you hugely in your career when you get to more advanced topics and realize that your base is weak in such an important tool.

Vectors are multidimensional numbers. In the section on physics we saw how important it is to grasp the concept of dimensions. Vectors and matrices are disciplines through which maths steps in to help solve multidimensional problems in physics. Our primary education starts with learning numbers and adding, subtracting, multiplying and dividing them. Vectors are the primary education for the new mathematics that you will be using in your engineering. The top tip in working with vectors is to always keep their geometric representation in your mind. You can see below an example of a geometric representation of dot and cross products.

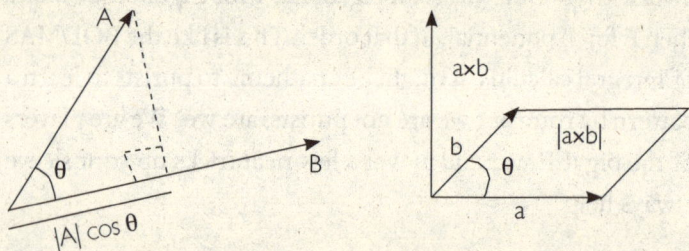

Mathematics in Summary

There are very few tips for JEE mathematics. It is the hardest of all the three subjects and I will have to admit that a certain natural ability is needed to get through it. Students start preparing for JEE very much in advance these days, some as early as class six. I strongly advise those who start early to invest all the extra time they have in mathematics. Practise problems like crazy. Get hold of correspondence material and textbooks from everywhere you can; just pick up problems and solve them. There is no substitute for practice in mathematics. Also learn from others as much as you can. You might be getting the correct answer, but someone else may be getting the same answer through a much smarter method. Even if you get the correct answer to a problem, look at the provided solution. Compare your solution with the standard solution and fine-tune the nuances, the little tricks that set a master apart from the amateur.

You will have to like maths because you will be spending a lot of time with it in your JEE preparation. If you are the kind of person who doesn't 'like' maths, please look for some other career option. However, if you like maths but only find it a little difficult, this can be sorted out through practice.

SIT THE EXAM RIGHT

88. An Exam-Friendly Strategy

You get marks for the knowledge you display inside the examination hall. Whatever you do for a whole year, however well you think you know a subject and however great your notes might be, if you don't write in that answer book what the examiners want you to write, you cannot score. So, always keep the exam in mind and never lose focus.

In most cases, joining some kind of tuition helps. Don't make tuitions the basis of your study plan though and don't join those that put too great a burden on you. Use tuitions to get tips and tricks for scoring in your exams. They will talk about patterns and make you do sample tests. They will give you early feedback and help you iron out your mistakes and develop strategies to rectify them. All this will help you develop a better understanding of what will and will not get you marks.

Tuitions are also an important source of competitive intelligence. Yes! Remember we are talking about topping your exams and not just about scoring well in them. Many of your competitors will also be coming to these tuitions and this gives you a way of assessing their preparation and the methods they are using. This is a good way to learn from other's methods and their mistakes, to compare your own preparation and sample test results with theirs. This can be done without joining tuitions as well if you are good at it, either through study groups or just by having a healthy relationship with your competitors.

Even if you don't go for tuitions, you must practise sample tests. If you solve the papers for the previous ten years for each subject, you will yourself see patterns in the way the JEE exams are designed. Don't make the mistake of trying to extrapolate and guess what specific questions might show up in this year's exam. Try to understand how the examiners aim to evaluate your grasp of the concepts. There are some important concepts that are always tested year after year.

There are some standard trick questions that keep showing up every now and then.

Prepare under the gun. Most of all, practise under pressure of time. Never read sample test papers at leisure, always write them under the 'time gun'. Some questions may look very easy when you are not thinking about the time but may actually take a lot of time when you get down to solving them. In my opinion, there is no direct correlation between the marks allocated to a question and the time it takes to solve it. Don't be surprised if you find a 2-mark question taking more time (generally because there is some clever trick involved, which may not come quickly to you) than a 4-mark question. Solve a few sample papers to get a feel of the marks allocated to the various questions and the approximate time the entire paper takes you. There has to be a well-defined strategy of navigating through them and scoring marks. For example, I always went first for those questions which could accumulate the maximum marks in the least time.* Any question I found difficult to understand on the first reading, I would immediately put aside for the next iteration. Yes, I (and most successful candidates I know) do papers in iterations. Most of them traverse through the same question paper at least twice or thrice during the exam, picking the easiest ones in the first iteration, then the tougher ones and finally the real tough cookies.

* Vivek.

Revision cycles. As the exam gets closer, revision cycles become very important. If you have to crack the exam, you can't keep wasting time revising the whole book or the complete notes again and again. Trust your mind. You are planning to top the exam. So you should start assuming you already know certain basics rather than keep on revising them. This is where the structure of your notes comes in handy. As you get closer to the exam, you should revise just the notes, then just the notes of notes and finally just the outline. Some of my closest friends and I were finally left with just a few sheets of paper that we just had to keep revising for about ten days before the JEE exam.* The first of those sheets was the complete syllabus, the second contained the concepts in which I was most prone to make mistakes and the last was a secret page about which I will talk later.

Over the years the JEE has experimented with a lot of exam formats, from objective (screening) and subjective (mains) to just two objective papers to 2013's mains (objective) and advanced (objective). Whatever may be the format, objective questions have always been part of the JEE exam. While at the conceptual level both objective and subjective formats are similar, objective questions test you additionally on speed, accuracy and your ability to pick the right questions. This section will give you a few tips and guidelines specific to the objective section.

* Vivek.

89. Exclusion Is the Key

My father, like most fathers, never really interfered in my studies or my methods of study (I suppose most fathers are result-oriented).* However, on the morning of the screening (objective) exam, standing outside the examination centre he couldn't help but give me a few tips. It was something that I knew all along, but coming from him made it special. The tip from my father, a doctor, who had no clue about any non-medical syllabus, was simple: this is an objective exam, so it is about exclusion not inclusion. Exclude questions you think you are not comfortable solving and when solving a question exclude options you know for sure are wrong. You do not have to solve each and every question. This is just a screening exam, it doesn't really matter what rank you get so do not stress about the quantity, just focus on quality.

So I entered the examination hall with only one thought—I do not have to do all the questions. I skipped questions at will and ended up going through all the questions in about 2 hours and 15 minutes. I spent another 30 minutes attempting questions that I had skipped. All this time I kept track of the number of questions that I had done in the first go and the number of questions that I attempted in the second round. I was extremely confident about the questions that I did in the first round and fairly confident about those that I attempted in the second round. I was happy with the number of questions

* Paras.

I had attempted so for the last 15 minutes, I did not try any new questions and just did a quick revision of whatever I had already done.

I walked out confident of what I had done and knew that I would make it to the mains. What this approach did was that it never let the exam pressure get to me. Ignoring what I did not know and just focusing on my strong points meant that I took the exam with the right focus. My focus was to make it to the mains and not bother about the rank in screening. All screening ranks from the top to the last 1.5 lakh are the same. This mindset made sure that I was calm and relaxed during the exam and never lost my nerve even if I wasn't able to answer a few questions.

The lesson here is to realize why you are sitting for the exam and what it is that you need to achieve. If it is a screening, your focus should be on getting through it (irrespective of the rank you get). However, if it is the final exam (mains or any other rank-deciding exam), you should first focus on doing what you know best, so that you clear the minimum cut-offs and are sure of getting some rank. Then you slowly move to your second-best topics and start building your rank.

90. Set Your Target Score

Before you sit for any objective-type examination, research the trend of the previous years to know what is a good score that can help get you in the selection list. Set yourself sectional (physics/chemistry/mathematics) and overall targets in terms of the number of questions that you need to get right to make it into the final list. Once you've done that, you must work towards improving your rank. Having a clear-cut target helps you pick and choose questions and keep a cool head. Once you have answered sufficient questions to near your target, you will naturally feel more confident, thereby increasing your chances of cracking tough questions as well.

Make sure you are cognizant of the sectional cut-offs as in JEE you need to clear the cut-offs for all the three sections separately. First on, your order of business should be to meet the sectional cut-offs and then move to your strongest subject to clear the overall cut-off and start building your rank. It is not a bad idea to start with your strongest subject and quickly do a few questions that will help you clear the sectional cut-off and then move on to the other subjects. Setting these targets helps you acquire clarity about what you need to achieve and thus you can plan better to reach your goal.

91. A Pause Will Not Kill You

Time is so limited that some people try to complete the entire paper in one single breath. I know of people who fainted midway during the JEE exam. Please understand, these are three hours of maximum possible pressure on your brain. More than two (maybe even four) years of mixing and grinding and cooking and now you are required to dish it all out neatly in just about a couple of hours, like a masterchef. Trust me, it might help to take half a minute's pause.

It helped me a lot. In every single exam that I have taken (and succeeded in) till date (this includes JEE, CAT, GATE and GMAT to boot), I have always taken an eyes-shut, two- to three-minute break in between.[*] I would just put the pen down, close my eyes, then open them and look left and right; it was almost like an out-of-body experience as I would see myself sitting in the hall, look back upon those hours and hours of toil and how that one hour right then was probably the most important hour of my life.

I strongly recommend a pause in the middle of the exam which recharges you and freshens you up. The remaining part of the exam then starts like a new exam, from scratch.

92. Eliminating Options

Objective exams generally have tight timelines and as such you need to be a little creative in how you approach them and solve them quickly. You will learn a lot of tricks over the next two years to solve objective problems fast. Till then, here is a list of tricks that I used:

1. Check the units/dimensions of the options. Force has unit of Newton or $Kg m/s^2$. Check for options that have wrong units like kg, m/s^2, etc., and quickly put a cross against them.

2. Substitute the solutions into the problem equation. If you are asked to solve an equation for (x,y), it is

---

[*] Vivek. GATE is the Graduate Aptitude Test in Engineering and GMAT is the Graduate Management Admission Test.

sometimes very quick to substitute the options given for (x,y) into the equation and see if the condition (equality or greater than or less than, etc.) holds.

3. Substitute angles in a trigonometric equation. For questions that ask you about whether a right-angled/ acute-angled/obtuse-angled triangle will satisfy a particular trigonometric equation, substitute the values of sin/cos/tan, etc., of various common angles such as 30, 60, 90, 120, etc. Keep a set of angles for acute/right/obtuse-angled triangles and their corresponding sin/cos/tan handy to quickly complete such questions.

4. For summation of various series put n=3 and quickly see which of the options gives you the right answer. No point solving the entire series and finding the sum.

5. Play at the boundaries. Test the boundary conditions for various equations. Test them at the boundaries of the given options and see if the conditions are satisfied or not.

93. Keep Track of Question Numbers

Almost all objective-type exams will ask you to fill in the answers in an OMR sheet (bubble sheet) using an HB pencil. The problem with this bubble sheet is that it is separate from the question paper and you have to fill all the answers in this sheet. This means you have to solve the question on one sheet and fill in the answer in a different sheet. Life is easy as long as you are attempting the questions serially and filling them on to the OMR sheet, but once you skip a few questions, the chances of filling the wrong bubble (filling the bubble for question no. 23 instead of 24, because you had skipped questions no. 20 to 25) go up significantly. Once you get one bubble wrong, chances are that the next five bubbles you fill will also be wrong. So take the utmost care while filling the answer bubbles. Once you have found out the answer to a problem, look at its question number and make sure you fill it in the right row in the OMR sheet. These few seconds of cautiousness will go a long way to avoid last-minute panic when you discover you have messed up the bubbles (that is, if you're able to notice this during the exam). Also, don't mix up the answer symbols (mark b instead of d). Always double-check that you've marked the answer that you intended.

Another common mistake students make is that they don't fill in the OMR sheet as soon as they solve the questions. They keep the task for the last 10 minutes. This is like suicide. In the last 10 minutes you will panic and are bound to make a few mistakes while filling the OMR. Also, with this approach there is a chance that you may not be able to fill the OMR for all the questions that you solved. So, not only is this method error-prone but it can also result in you missing out on questions you had solved correctly. *Do not postpone filling the OMR sheet.* Ideally, you should fill it after solving every question. However, you can also choose to fill the bubbles every ten minutes or so. During the last 15 minutes of the exam, though, mark the OMR as soon as you solve each question.

94. Pen or Pencil?

Stick to the pencil for everything, because too much time, energy and focus is wasted in switching between pen (used for solving questions) and pencil (used for filling the OMR). That gives you too many things to deal with on a small desk, so avoid the hassle, keep life simple and stick to the pencil. This also eliminates the risk of filling the OMR bubble with a pen by mistake.

95. Round Off Numbers

If the options are not very close, you can round off the numbers and then quickly do the calculation. This will save you a lot of time. But you have to be cautious while using this approach for questions whose answer options are very close to each other. No rounding off is generally the best policy, but you have to take it on a case-by-case basis. Also make sure you know whether you'll be underestimating or overestimating the answer when you round off a numerator or denominator.

CRACK IT!

I don't know whether it's fair to test all the hard work and effort of two years in one day, but that's how JEE works. This the day you have waited for, to put to test all that you have learnt, to write one final time the alphas, betas and gammas of the science that is the JEE syllabus. There are no set rules on what to do in the last few days, but here are a few suggestions you may find useful.

96. Simulate the JEE Environment

JEE, like most exams, starts at around 8 a.m. or 9 a.m. and continues till around 5 p.m. This means that you will have to wake up at around 5 a.m. and leave for the examination centre by say 7 a.m. Now, this is pretty early by any standards and so it is better to condition yourself for this ordeal. While you may think that there is nothing that can come in your way and you will be at your best irrespective of what time you get up and how much you have to travel, the truth is that your body can and will react to a sudden change in routine and you do not want to lose even 1 per cent of your performance and efficiency. Thus, it is best to not leave this routine adjustment for the final day as there will be plenty to deal with on that day and you don't want to feel sleepy or have nausea set in.

It is important especially for the student who prefers reading in the night to change his schedule at least a month prior to the exam date so that his body has sufficient time to adjust to the change and perform at its optimum levels. Make sure you start getting up early, finish your daily chores by 7 a.m. and start your studies by 9 a.m.

Students often find it difficult to eat something this early in the morning. It is important that you overcome these challenges either by a change in routine or by improvising (keeping some chocolates handy). For competitive exams like

JEE, you need to be at your peak during the exam hours; one of the ways in which you can do it is to simulate the exam conditions and attempt mock JEE exams in the exact hours during which they will be held on the exam day. Make sure you sit for at least three hours at a stretch and get yourself into the examination groove. Simulate the examination hall— remember, no air conditioners (maybe not even fans if the electricity board has its way), no refreshments, no breaks, no music playing in the background. It should be just you and an exam sheet and everything else should just fade away.

97. Take It Easy

'*Ho gayi taiyari?*' (Are you well-prepared?) I'm sure you and your friends have asked each other this question before every exam. And I can bet my money and say that the answer was always an emphatic 'NO'. I am yet to find someone who is supremely confident of having done enough preparation for an exam. There is always that last-minute hustle to get a handle on one more concept or have another look at the formulas or maybe one last round of a quick revision of key concepts. Exam preparation is a never-ending journey and you pick up steam right before the finish line, in this case the exam date.

However, there is a slight difference between JEE and the school exams for which you have appeared till now. While the school exams test you on one subject at a time and include syllabus subjects from only one year, JEE tests you on three subjects with the syllabus spanning over two years. Also, unlike school exams, there is no set pattern for JEE examination, so you cannot really predict beyond a certain level what the questions will be. You have to treat JEE like a marathon and not a sprint like the school exams. A marathon requires you to train consistently and slowly build your strength and stamina so that you can last the entire distance. A last-minute sprint will only get you as far as maybe 200 metres and then you will fall flat on your face and your race will be over before it actually begins. For JEE, just like a marathon preparation, you should take ample rest before the big day.

So, take it easy in the last week. Do some light reading over the week and do not study one day before the exam. There are just too many things to cover and the more you read the more you will doubt your preparation. Your mind will have worked like a machine in the weeks leading up to the exam and is quite likely to be exhausted by now. So, give it a break and do not overload information into it one day before the main exam. Let your mind calm down. Trust yourself and your hard work of the past two years. Believe in yourself and your preparation. You have studied all that there was to be studied and one day is not going to make any difference (it may actually make you more anxious). So, on the eve of the exam take out time to sit with your family, watch a movie on TV, listen to some music, etc. In short, just relax. Put your admit card, pencil box and other requirements in place. Remember to sleep early.

98. No New Topics Now

Like I said, preparing for JEE is like preparing for a marathon. You stick to a routine and slowly build stamina. You experiment when you start preparing but do not try too many new things closer to the race day. You'll do your best by sticking to the basics and following your routine. The last few weeks are the worst time to pick up a new topic (unless it is a very small topic and you are confident of cracking it). Even if you pick up a new topic in the last month, you will not be able to delve deep into it and practise enough variations of the concept. Your knowledge and confidence in that topic will be average at best and chances are that average will not make the cut in the JEE exam.

This is the time when you should focus on revising the known concepts and getting a synopsis of the entire two years of studying. It is the time when you go through all the concepts, look at a few problems from each topic and refresh your memory with a quick reading of all the rules and principles. If you start a new topic in the last week, you will lose out on revising other concepts where a mere revision is bound to get you close to 100 per cent accuracy. Thus, the choice is between dealing with a known devil and an unknown devil. My advice is to pick the known devil and try to tame it rather than wander into a new territory against an unknown adversary.

Leave the topic that you have ignored for the past two years and make peace with the fact that you will have to ignore the related questions if they crop up in the final exam. In the last few weeks, it is better to play within your circle of comfort and try to play better than everybody else. The bigger question is whether you should ignore a topic and keep it pending till the last month. The ideal answer is, of course not. But JEE, because of its competition and vast and related syllabus, gives you some room to play with the topics that you may want to ignore and yet be confident of making it to the IITs.

99. Ignore What You Don't Know

JEE is a long exam and has a lot of questions. However, a glance at the cut-offs will show you that it's not an exam where you have to solve each and every question. A lot of people make it to the IITs by solving just a limited number of questions. One of the rules that you have to remember is that cracking JEE is not about solving each and every problem; it's about targeting the problems you are confident about and solving them correctly. Sometimes it happens that you might get stuck on a problem which you feel you can solve and then you end up wasting a lot of time on it. The general rule of thumb is to keep moving forward. You don't want to be in a situation where you spend too much time on one question and then race against time for the rest of the exam. In such a situation, you start to lose your calm and increase the chances of goof-ups. Be selective about the questions you begin with. It will help you settle in easily, boost your confidence and help you keep a calm and composed head during the rest of the paper.

In a pen-and-paper exam, you can put marks against questions that you may want to attempt in the second go. Another great tool is to mark the questions differently as per the difficulty or your comfort level with the topic. You can use a star-marking scheme or a much quicker one-dash, two-dash and cross (for something that you won't attempt till the end) system—I recommend the latter because time is of the essence, and stars take too much time. This will make sure that you attempt questions in the order of your comfort and preparation.

Pace yourself well throughout the exam. Don't spend a lot of time initially on questions that you feel are taking too long. I have heard a lot of people say that they will spend 90 of the 180 minutes on maths and only 30 minutes in the end on chemistry because maths is tough and requires a lot of time. While you may have a basis (past test performances, etc.) for this time division, keeping the subject with which you are most comfortable and are quick at for the end may not be a good strategy. If you are so confident that you can finish off a particular subject quickly, do that first. It will give you a lot of confidence going into the next section and also ensure that you don't lose out time on the subject where you can score most comfortably. Always keep track of time and never get engrossed in a question for long.

100. Do Not Discuss the Exam Midway

In its latest avatar, the JEE exam has two parts of three hours each. There is a two-hour break between the two exams. You will leave the examination centre after Part One and are free to go out, eat, and so on. This break is a crucial time to recharge your batteries, take some rest and get your focus back. It is a time to get ready for the final bout. You have to make sure that you utilize this break optimally to prepare yourself for the next part of the examination.

Stay away from the frenzy. There will be a lot of commotion outside the examination centre, especially with parents asking their children how they did in the exam. Random people will ask you if the exam was tough. It's understandable that there will be a lot of anxiety among the parents and other students but the last thing you want to do is to get caught in this frenzy and start thinking about how well you performed in the first part. No matter what you do during this break, *do not discuss the exam with anyone*. Do not go looking for your friends and start asking how their exam went. Do not seek answers to any particular question. Do not answer random people about whether the exam was tough or one section was tricky or not. Ask your parents to not bother you with similar questions. You do not want to suddenly realize that you might have made a silly mistake and keep obsessing about it during the next part.

Nothing good will come from knowing that you've made a silly mistake or that your answers do not match with your friends'. In case some of the answers do not match, you will feel you've already lost a chance and the game is over. Or it will put undue pressure on you to crack the second exam. Your mind will start going wild and all this when no one knows the right answer. It is best to believe that whatever you have done is right and just focus on the next part.

Just remember, what you did in there you did to the best of your knowledge and ability. So why compare, especially when there is another exam coming up in a couple of hours? Forget about Part One the moment you step out of the hall. Don't take part in the commotion outside the examination centre. Go to your parents, sit somewhere quiet and relax and sip some juice. Use the break to regain your mental energy and focus on the next paper. Make sure you eat something (not too heavy) during this time. If you're one of those who can afford some sleep during this time, believe me, it's the best preparation for the next exam.

Life and IIT

WHAT IF?

The biggest fear in the minds of most JEE aspirants is 'What if I do not get selected?' Everybody has some backup plan or the other. The most common approach is to appear for a few other entrance exams such as All India Engineering Entrance Examination (AIEEE), various state institutions, such as Delhi College of Engineering, and select reputed private colleges, such as Birla Institute of Technology and Science. It is not a bad approach; if you don't become an engineer from IIT, at least you will become an engineer. However, you have to be very clear that this is what you want. Some students also go to the extent of taking seats in these colleges, including the IITs with lower ranks and then reappear for the JEE the next year for a second shot. Though not a great approach, you are entitled to your take. My question is, if you have to sweat so much to get into an IIT, is it worth it? Don't get me wrong, but maybe you should have an open mind and evaluate other career options as well. There are some very good courses in science, there are design institutes and there are options for degrees abroad. It might not be entirely wasteful to talk to a career counsellor for more help on these options. Don't get needlessly stuck on IIT-JEE. It is not the only key to heaven any more; there are many paths to getting there.

MOMENT OF TRUTH . . . AND JOY

You follow all these hundred tips—and perhaps a thousand more of your own—to increase your chances. Then of course your standing in the spiritual world also counts. For instance, for Hindu students, not a single Tuesday is missed in the sequence of trips to a Hanuman temple, not an eyelash missed in wishing off from the back of your hand, not a single train missed when passing under a bridge—not one, as you never know which one might make that crucial difference. Then there are your near and dear ones—your mother most of all I would assume—sending prayers upwards on your behalf. When all of this has fallen into place, when it has been ordained by heaven and earth, by friend and foe and by thought, word and deed that 'Yes! YOU are the chosen one!' you finally get yourself a pass through the Pearly Gates. It doesn't come easy, and so when it comes it hits you like crazy. The mental conditioning we have discussed earlier becomes extremely important at this point.

When I had my pass in my hand, I was over the moon.[*] The good part of growing up in a small town is that the dreams are small, the expectations are fewer and hence the joys are that much bigger. Given who I thought I was, and given what I had put into my preparation, getting in was probably the best-case scenario. I don't remember ever thinking about any rank per se. It was just a Bernoulli trial with only two possible outcomes.

A side note about one of my friends: he never missed a chance to pour into my ears the gory details of how prepared everyone else was and who was likely to get what rank. At the end of his news updates he would condescendingly let me know that I was also likely to be in the top 500. I would blush and be coy, eventually ending up just plain confused and, I admit, scared of my peers. I never really put a number to my dreams, though now with the benefit of hindsight I know most people do. After hearing from my friend about the likely rank of every single aspirant from Allahabad, I did some relative positioning and evaluated my best-case scenario to be a rank in the top 500. The probability I gave myself for that was so low that impossible is the only descriptive substitute for that number. Given this shallow amniotic sac of expectations in which my brain was floating, it was probably natural for it to burst in joy when the news was broken to me.

I got a call from my study partner that a certain local

* Vivek.

coaching centre had the results. We cycled to that place, encouraging each other with butterflies in our stomachs. When I reached there I remember someone shouting my name, announcing that I had arrived. I went into a tizzy. I was busily ushered inside to a small, dark room where seated at a table with two telephones on his desk and one by his ear was a person I rightly guessed to be the owner of the coaching centre. The news was broken to me that I was the chosen one that year, netting the highest rank in my town. Pats on the back, congratulatory words all around—dream sequence. I went and sat down in the middle of the road outside, soaking in the moment. I rushed back home and shared the news with my family. It was raining. I rushed to the roof and soaked myself in the downpour. I was happy . . . for a while, at least.

DREAMS AND REALITY

Then came the other part—the part where this over-the-moon-happiness gives way to confusion and disillusionment. Dreams mostly outdo reality when it comes to creative simplicity and beauty. My brain had modelled an IIT campus on the lines of *Jo Jeeta Wohi Sikandar* and *Shola aur Shabnam*; both these movies had a pretty significant college backdrop and had released about the same time as I was preparing for the JEE. I always imagined lots of bicycles, lots of colourful dresses, a brilliant and vibrant campus with lots and lots of students walking about, chatting under the trees. When I came face-to-face with the Kanpur campus, the only part of this concoction finally realized was the trees.

COUNSELLING: MAJOR VS CAMPUS

In case you don't know, 'major' here refers to the specialization you choose to go for in an IIT, that is, mechanical or computers or textile, etc. 'Campus' refers to the specific IIT campus you decide to join. So, the debate is about whether your decision should be based on which specialization you want or which IIT you want to go to?

Counselling is a misnomer, not just at the IITs, but in most competitive exams in India in general. These so-called counselling venues are not very different from a medieval fish market where you enter with a certain rank in your pocket and hope to get the best value for your 'goods'. The relative ranking of the various courses across the different colleges is mostly predetermined and a student's own counselling has probably already happened through his relatives and friends even before he enters the venue. The scene at these counselling venues resembles that inside a stock exchange in some sense. There are huge electronic billboards that keep displaying the going rank for each specific department after each round of counselling is over. Students are anxiously keeping track of this and feverishly chattering away with counselling advisers, appointed seniors and fellow applicants for instant advice.

It is indeed odd how one can be expected to receive counselling related to his entire career and life, ponder over it, and take a decision amidst dynamic billboards sequentially shutting off doors creating an atmosphere of near panic and commotion. When I was filling my top three choices for the courses I wanted to take, I realized for the first time how little I had thought about this in the past two years. *I had spent two years thinking about an exam and had forgotten to think about my life.* Counselling, as it is popularly called in India, is a joke. It is no more than an auction. And, to be fair, with so many vying for such few seats, I don't think institutions have the resources to make these sessions any better. So, the onus is essentially on you to get all your counselling done before you get called for the official IIT-JEE counselling.

At eighteen years of age, not many students are sure of what course they want and which IIT they should choose. Frankly, when you have studied maths and science for the last fifteen years of your academic life, courses like biotechnology, electrical engineering, computers, etc., all sound unfamiliar and you cannot really judge which one you will like and will enjoy studying. When I went into the counselling session, I was as clueless as the others around me. I had spoken to my older cousins and sought opinions from my seniors, but in the end it was left to me. What complicates matters is the fact that you not only have to choose the major but also have to earmark an IIT as your preferred choice. While almost all IITs were at an equal footing some ten years back, the number of new IITs that have come up have created a belief that the more established and older IITs may actually be better than the newer ones.

In a way, counselling is perhaps the first time ever that you're going to make a big decision that has a strong correlation with the kind of work you might end up doing for a major chunk of your life. So, take your time, talk to as many peers and seniors as you can. Tell them what you like and dislike. Tell them what you want out of your job (a vague idea may be good enough). Ask them if they think they made the right choices and if not, what they would have considered if they were to make that decision again.

Things you should not consider while making the decision:

1. *Relative distance from your home.* While it is great to be in an IIT closer to your home, it should not be a factor driving your choice. Your parents, like all parents, may want to have you nearby but the chances of you visiting home during the term are low. After the first year you wouldn't really want to go home and would much rather plan trips with your friends.

2. *Third cousin of your neighbour took branch X and is doing great.* Taking advice is great, but it is important to take advice from the right people. Just because some unknown person went to a particular IIT and a particular branch doesn't make it the right choice for *you.* Ignore advice that doesn't have a sound footing.

3. *Branch X is the future.* There is only so much that one

can predict about the future. Do not pay heed when people say that the future will belong to this field and that subject. Don't choose your major because someone believes it's going to be the next big thing in a decade or so. While it is great to have a futuristic view that has a strong foundation, one shouldn't really make a career choice based entirely on such a prediction.

Remember, whatever IIT you choose and whichever course you choose, you will never be 100 per cent sure that you made the right choice. Still, you can rest assured that it will not be the be all and end all of your professional life. Chances are that the work you end up doing will have very little to do with the course you took at IIT. So, I'll say it again, take your time, figure out what matters to you, create your value metrics and then take the plunge. Are you ready?

Let me assume for a moment that you are not someone in class eleven or twelve. I want you to assume that you have already been selected for IIT and that you have the best rank you possibly could. Which course and which IIT would you choose? Would it be textile engineering from IIT Delhi or electrical engineering from IIT Madras or would it be computer engineering from IIT Kanpur? Once you have made this choice, ask yourself—'Why did I make this choice?' Do you know what you will be taught in the first year? Do you know what are the pros and cons of each of these courses? Do you know the career prospects of a computer engineer versus a textile engineer? In fact, the bigger question is—Do you care?

I say this from experience.* As soon as I was selected, my dad took me to a senior professor in our local engineering college for advice on which stream I should choose. The professor didn't think twice before categorically recommending electrical engineering for me. He went on to espouse the virtues of the discipline and the fact that electrical engineers in any case end up learning computer engineering but not vice-versa. The merit in his arguments did not bear as much upon me as his persona itself—he had the aura of a maestro. From that moment on I was convinced beyond doubt that electrical engineering was my future. This conviction stayed and firmed up within me for thirty days before I reached the counselling venue.

I went to the counselling venue with my sister and brother-in-law. While I was filling the forms inside and chatting with would-be batchmates, a stranger prompted my brother-in-law that it would be fairly stupid to give up computer science with a rank of 69. He must definitely have had some force in his argument, because I got called out of the room promptly and was told about the new insight. Somehow, the erstwhile aura of the professor paled before the aura of that stranger, which was amplified by the aura of my brother-in-law, and I ended up changing my choice to computer science.

Of course, this caused only a little drama in my life because fortunately my rank was strong. But having been

* Vivek.

through the counselling drama with some of my other friends later on, I have seen how such an important decision is taken in haste and chaos. My advice to you would be to take counselling very seriously, prepare in advance and not leave it to the last moment.

THINK FOR YOURSELF

Here is my recipe to avoid all this confusion: talk to experienced people. I know there are lots of motivational, inspirational and biographical books available, which a lot of people read. My own father was a huge fan of Swami Vivekananda and badgered me to read his works.* To please him I bought a biography and a full-length poster of the great Swami and hung it in my room. How my dad beamed in appreciation! Did I admire and get inspired by Vivekananda? Sure! Did I get any practical advice about my career from Vivekananda? Not really! Because the Vivekanandas, Einsteins, Edisons and Ramanujams lived in a different time. What they did or said will have to be interpreted and can be adapted only at a very abstract level for our day-to-day lives. But talking to someone living next door, who has fought the same battles as you are fighting—for example, someone who has actually studied engineering at IIT Delhi—is far more valuable when thinking about your life ahead. Keep talking

* Vivek.

173

to people who have the benefit of hindsight. It will mould your thoughts and give them structure. Gradually, you will start seeing things clearly. And, who knows, amidst that clarity you may suddenly have that moment of truth about what you really want to do. Trust me, 99 per cent of people who want you to get into an IIT have never been there. All that has changed is that in 1992 Aamir Khan had us believe that every college was like the one in *Jo Jeeta Wohi Sikandar* and in 2009 he had us believe it is like the one in *Three Idiots*. The simplification and generalization is still grossly endemic. What you need is your own version of life at IIT, not anyone else's version of it. Build your own understanding of what a seat at IIT really means to you before you commit your life to it.

GAME PLAN

Like JEE, IIT is also to be pursued with a clear game plan. Once you get selected, there is not much time left, so it is better to have the game plan in mind sooner rather than later. I would lay out the broad contours of this game plan in terms of the four years you have to spend to get your degree.

Personality Development Programme

A word on the Personality Development Programme (PDP) is in order here. It lasts only for a month or so but the memories it leaves behind last forever. Trust me, PDP will be one of the biggest tests of your personality and one of your best opportunities to make friends. It is a good time to gauge how tough you are. You will need to be tough to get through IIT and through life after IIT, so take PDP as a personality test and approach it with a positive and open mind.

Good or Bad?

I got my first flavour of PDP on the counselling day itself.* For some reason I can't remember, I went for a walk to one of the hostels. A gang of my seniors was waiting for me. Now think about this—counselling happens in summer, which is supposed to be vacation-time for students. Then what were these students doing in the hostel? I had no time to ponder over these details. The seniors were all over me within minutes. The interesting thing about PDP is that you are on the receiving side of the table only once and on the other side of the table thrice in your life. From that point of view, most of us begin to tacitly support PDP as something largely innocuous. But ask the student who faces it for the first time—there is never any fun in it. Strangers from nowhere toy with your values, your background and your dignity. No matter how benign and friendly they may try to be, it can never be fun. I will admit that during my own PDP period there were a few good moments with some interesting and jovial seniors, but on the

* Vivek.

whole it was a distasteful experience. It is annoying, intrusive and interferes thoroughly with your efforts to settle into your new life. So, in my first PDP session, I was petrified. Those seniors seemed to have so much power that I felt they could actually do anything. I still remember that with them was a student with East Asian features whom they kept referring to as 'Bodo', and they kept hinting that he always carried a kukri in his pants. Bodo eventually became a friend and we went to our first job together, and all those seniors who were PDPing me that day also became very good friends. But on that day they really had me believe that Bodo had a kukri in his pants. When they took me for a walk to those desolate, semi-arid zones of IIT Kanpur behind Hall 3 (now of course those areas have swanky new buildings), I remember very clearly the moment when I really feared the kukri was going to come out and stab me in my ribs. So, yes, PDP is scary and takes its toll on your psyche. (Of course now I laugh at how naive and stupid I was back then to be scared of those people.)

Surviving PDP

The key is to relax. Nobody is going to kill you. With so many tough regulations in place, they are as scared of doing something serious as you are. Don't get carried away by threats. They are mostly just saying things to mess with you; they don't mean any of it. The test is of your ability to take things with a pinch of salt. Personal jokes are the most common cause of serious psychological damage. If something like that happens, you can start getting angry but avoid losing your temper completely. My first reaction used to be to just grin, somewhat seriously, and tell them, 'Sir, please don't say these things.' Trust me, they got the hint that I was not taking it as a joke. They are not your enemies, but they also don't know the limits of your sense of humour. So keep telling them if you are getting uncomfortable and keep your wits and sense of humour about you. A sullen look is the harbinger of bad omens in PDP. Some tips for surviving PDP—be talented and resourceful, because these are the two kinds of people I have seen breezing through PDP quite easily. The talents that work best are singing and mimicry. The resources that are most sought after are charm and cigarettes. If you can pull these out of your hat, you will be welcomed. It might actually be a good idea to develop some acts or learn some songs in the days between your selection and your counselling.

The First Year

This year the mantra should be to dig your heels in. A violent storm is about to hit you in the first year, so if your heels are not dug in deep you will just get blown away. It will be a completely new experience for most of you. There will be the hostel experience, the late-night Maggi, the early-morning hustle to reach class on time, the rare all-nighter for studies and fun. To survive and to get the most out of your first year and lay a solid foundation for the next three years, you have to balance the two aspects—relationships and academics.

Relationships have to be made strong with the following stakeholders, in the given order of priority—peers, seniors and faculty. Forget about your family; they will not be around. Even if you fly home four times a month to hug and kiss them, it is useless because the moment the clock strikes 7 a.m. on a Monday morning, no one from your family will be there to help you. If you have school friends or girlfriends back home who stood by you through thick and thin during the last two years, thank them but don't expect them to help you any more. Your peers, that is, your classmates, are all you will have for friends and family for the next four years. Your friends are going to be the ones who are going to have fun with you, make fun of you, fight with you, fight for you, stand by you when things go bad, leave you stranded to make you feel stupid and more.

I am no guru on relationships (quite the opposite, actually) but I can tell you one mantra that works best to build relationships with peers—'Give respect and do things together'. Respect is a two-way street and if you don't give respect, there is no hope for you to get any. Each of your peers is equally smart and will not take it well if you don't respect them. This does not mean that you cannot have fun with them or tease them, but you'll have to maintain the fine line between having fun and hurting people. The IITs are a collaborative environment and doing things together will help you build long-lasting relationships. Don't be the person who is ultra-competitive, doesn't share notes and important information with others. Doing this may get you good marks but will not get you any respect from your peers and, believe me, grades will help you go only so far in life. So help your friends and be happy for their triumphs.

Doing things together does not mean drinking, smoking and watching movies on the LAN—at least not just that. Doing things together also means participating in cultural and sports events, going for jogs and to the gym, maybe even going to the library together. Also, try to have as broad a circle as possible. Of course you will have a few close friends, but that should not mean you don't hang out with others. Seniors at IIT work differently than seniors in most other colleges. Saying 'Sir-Sir' and bending over double doesn't help. Being a 'fundoo guy' helps. The more active you are in events in the hostel or institute, the better you will fare with your seniors.

Lastly, you need to manage your relationships with your professors in IIT—what they love the most in first-year students is discipline. In fact, by being disciplined you actually maintain your relationships with the faculty as well as shore up your defences in academics. Keep it simple: show up on time in class, stay attentive and submit your assignments on time. Easier said than done! Ask any student in IIT and he will tell you that not more than 5 per cent of all students in a class are actually able to adhere to this for the first two semesters. Forget about the grades. If you are disciplined enough to show up on time for classes and are able to sit attentively through them, the grades will take care of themselves.

The most important part is to keep the equation of relationships and academics balanced. The moment this equality becomes an inequality your smooth curve of progress will degenerate to a singularity and you will fall off the IIT grid. A simple rule of thumb is that your final grades (at least till placements) ought to be very close to the grades you end up with after the first year. The cumulative nature of grading ensures that it gets progressively difficult to improve or indeed ruin one's grades as the terms progress.

The Second Year

This is by far the most exciting year at IIT because by now you will have settled well into the system and any apprehensions that you may have had in the beginning will be gone. You will be comfortable in the environment and will not be shy to express yourself and make full use of the IIT facilities to enjoy yourself. This is generally the year where studies take a back seat and one's focus shifts to exploring new things (tennis, dance, SPIC MACAY, etc.).

While this year promises a lot of fun, it is also the year where most people lose their way. The horror stories that you may have heard about students turning into drunkards, flunking the entire year, getting semester bans, etc., generally start from this year. So, make sure you make some room for your academics between all the fun.

I am stressing this because it is generally at the end of the second year that you realize you are in no man's land with respect to having a clear career goal, a respectable CGPA, outstanding extracurricular performance, etc. If your second year goes according to the average second year at IIT (which is to say on everything else but studies), I am sure you will feel directionless after the fourth term. Use the second year to figure out or at least start thinking about what you want from your IIT experience and what after IIT. I say this because by the end of this year if you have not decided (or at least started thinking about) what you want to do afterwards, you will feel lost and your confidence will take a hit.

Start the second year with the clear objective that at the end of this year you should have figured out where you want to end up after IIT and maybe where you want to be when you are thirty-five years old. Your options are academics, public service, private service and entrepreneurship. Each one of these options needs dedicated investment of time and energy, so you can't keep all the options open after the second year.

Now, how would you figure all this out in one year? The good news is that you have listened to advice in your first year and you have some awesome seniors and professors to discuss these things with. And, when all else fails, there is Google! In fact, whenever I say seniors from now on, include Google in that. Start speaking to your final-year seniors. If possible, hang out with them in the canteens or libraries. And, be patient; don't go around annoying them with basic questions. The gyan will rub off on you if you are observant and absorbent. Spend time getting inside the skin of the people whose shoes you want to fill within a couple of years. Ask them what options you can explore after IIT, what are the pros and cons of each of those options and how you should go about preparing yourself for these options.

A quick low-down on the four options I gave you: academics means research and teaching. For an IITian, it is usually much more research than teaching. You will have to go for at least another six years of campus life after you pass out of IIT. That is poison to some ears, honey to others. Figure out which type of ears you have. It also means you have to know which are the best places to spend those years. Places get very specific—it is not just a college but a lab or a research group. Seniors and professors can tell you whether machine learning systems research is done best at the University of Illinois at Urbana-Champaign or whether computational chemistry research is done best at Johns Hopkins, etc. You won't understand more than a cent of a dollar right now, but stay patient and let it keep hitting you. Gradually, you will get what you need.

Public service is not just the IAS. It is also not necessarily a government job. Public service refers to any position where the common people and their day-to-day problems are your problem. So, it could also be an NGO. And an NGO can be as big as the United Nations! Public service is music to the ears of people who are interested in the world outside of books and offices. There are eyes that water and burn when they see injustice and there are eyes that just roll. Which type are your eyes? Once you have used this sorting hat to become sure about public service, there is a 99 per cent chance that you are thinking of the IAS. Nothing wrong with it; it continues to be a tremendous career possibility in India. Spend time with seniors and on the Internet figuring out what goes into the preparation. It is usually a marathon of two or three years rather than a dash of six months (unlike the CAT / GRE / GMAT). Are you up to it? Which subjects will you choose to appear for the IAS entrance? The clearer you are on these things, the more accomplished your second year will be.

A private service job is the easiest option and also the most ambiguous one. A job is defined in four dimensions—industry, role, position and salary. Industry could be automotive, IT, BFSI (banking, financial services and insurance), etc. The one that is right for you is a function largely of the discipline you have chosen and the grades you have got. Technology and finance industries welcome graduates from any department with open arms as long as the person has proven himself in academics. Other industries are a little more conservative. Your role could be that of a tech geek, a suave manager, a street-smart sales executive, an influential marketer, or a number-crunching financial analyst. Positions could range from the entry-level to middle management to chief executive. And you certainly don't need me to tell you about the salary. In a private service job, the most important thing to understand is that the success curve, or the 'corporate ladder' as they call it, is anything but linear.

There is so much gyan that your seniors and the world are bound to give you on this that I will say only this much—your IIT badge is an evergreen one, but it begins to fade a little with the years. So, choose a job or role where you will naturally excel and not have to depend on your badge to take you far. A top-notch business-school badge is less important for an IITian than being in a profession that he will excel in. So, before you dive into your CAT preparations, be sure that you have figured out at least three or four awesome job options for yourself.

Entrepreneurship is the hottest option these days and also the one most suited for an IITian, in my opinion. If you want to be an entrepreneur, there is one thing you should definitely not do and that is think up a hundred business ideas every day and keep inflicting them on your peers and seniors. Either you will end up annoying them or they will end up demotivating you. Either way, your personal relationships will be at risk. An entrepreneurial career is suited for someone who can think of doing nothing else and who believes in his idea. It is in the DNA, it is genetic. Don't try to be an entrepreneur just because it sounds exciting. To understand what it's all about, read the biographies of successful businessmen like Steve Jobs, Bill Gates, J.R.D. Tata and Captain G.R. Gopinath. Inspiration is the key so find it early.

The Third Year

Your third year is about putting into action the decision you have taken in the second year. I will say this again—don't worry about grades. Just stay disciplined. The moment you start poking your nose into other people's CPA and setting a target for yourself you will create stress due to the gap between expectation and reality and mess up your disciplined approach to academics. Just show up in class, be attentive and do your assignments on time. Let the grades take care of themselves. In this way, your academics are on autopilot, cruise-control mode. And you can now look at your career, your life beyond IIT.

Projects and internships are the most important aspects of the third year. They are an opportunity to forge long-term relationships. Foreign internships will give you a chance to experience new cultures and work in some really great research labs. I have often found that students are more focused on landing a foreign internship for the prestige attached to it and don't really care if it matches their interests or not. Don't go for an internship just for the sake of it. Try for those internships which will add value to your overall plan. Those of you who are interested in research as a career should read about the various laboratories in the field of your interest and talk to your professors about which labs you should consider for internship. If you are focused on a job in a particular industry, go for an industrial internship. Taking up an internship in tandem with your interest will give you more clarity about what to expect after IIT.

Consider your project guide and faculty members as mentors and discuss your career goals with them. I firmly believe that of all the resources at IIT, students tend to underutilize the faculty the most. Most of the students shy away from the faculty because they fear being rebuked for not attending classes or some mischief or another. Rest assured you are not the first batch that your professors have taught. They are familiar with all the antics you can possibly think of. They have seen it all but are still very eager to help provided you treat them with respect. Put aside your fears and walk up to your professors to seek guidance on what career to choose and how to reach the top in that profession. IIT is nothing but the sum total of the people inside its walls. And the faculty are by far the smartest of those people, contrary to what you may on occasion think of them.

The second most important thing in the third year is the next set of exams you have to prepare for: CAT, GMAT, GRE (Graduate Record Examinations), TOEFL (Test of English as a Foreign Language) and IAS, among others. There are also many other company-specific entrance exams like those of SAIL (Steel Authority of India), ONGC (Oil and Natural Gas Corporation), HAL (Hindustan Aeronautics Limited), BHEL (Bharat Heavy Electricals), etc. The key to these competitive examinations is formulating your preparation strategy and finding time to execute it. The first part you will figure out for yourself when the time comes, but the second part, finding the time, is a little tricky. In your third year the academic load is killing, projects are pouring in wholesale, cultural events demand greater responsibility from you, and there are the demands of maintaining your relationships with your peer group. You have to ruthlessly separate the grain from the chaff. If there is a course where you will have to invest four hours a day to get from a C to a B, bite the bullet and settle for a C. If there is a project partner who is making you do the work for you both, while he plays Counter-Strike, come down very hard on him and don't shy away from reporting the matter and changing partners. If your friend is a fool who is ruining his own prospects as well as yours by watching movies and playing games every single night, cold-shoulder him and focus on your own interests. If you are not brutal about your time, time will be brutal to you.

The Final Year

I can hear the deep sighs. The bye-bye year when there is nothing left to fight for, when you want to extract the last drop of juice from the IIT canes, when best friends have become enemies and life has come full circle. People actually feel so old in the fourth year that it is hard for them to accept that their lives are actually going to start now. According to me, the fourth year should be all about tying up loose ends and rejuvenation. Close the loops in your relationships by saying things you wanted to say to people—seal positive relationships with an extra dose of gratitude and the negative ones by a good, friendly, not-the-end-of-the-world cup of tea. Unburden your load of regret, if any. Think of the good that will stick to you when you leave and try to shrug off any dirt you may have picked up. Redeem and relaunch yourself.

On a very serious note, make sure you don't ruin your chances with some rash act of stupidity in the last lap. I have seen people snap and I am warning you against it. Don't snap in the last lap because now is not the time. You have to thank your stars that you've got this far and take a little responsibility in seeing things through.

Placements

Placements are the process of placing students in suitable jobs at the end of their education. It is different from recruitment in that recruitment is finding the right candidate for a job, while placement is finding the right job for a candidate. This distinction is very important.

Placements in colleges today are gravitating towards a free, capitalistic job market. The students with the best grades mostly have the best jobs coming to them. The students with the worst grades don't always have jobs being offered to them. It is a classic demand–supply situation and the dynamics of the market roughly follow the contours of the Gale-Shapley algorithm (that got Shapley the Noble Prize for Economics in 2012). Different kinds of rules exist in various IITs to 'make' the process 'fair', which is a euphemism for giving a socialistic hue to an inherently capitalistic process. Every year, one a new rule is introduced because the new student placement coordinator and the administrative head of placement cannot be at peace until they have brought some changes in the system; it is part of their resume, after all. So, all in all, how exactly do placements differ from IIT to IIT and year to year?

The standard currency for this market is grades. Don't get the companies or the system wrong. We all know that at times grades don't represent true ability. However, for an outside entrant to this market (that is, the companies) it is the only standard proxy available and hence they have to strongly rely upon it. This is where you will reap the benefits if you have walked the talk on discipline. I have said very clearly earlier that you should not chase grades, but that does not mean that you abandon them. You just stay regular and keep up so that you end up with the grades you deserve.

Given your grades, there will be a natural selection process using which the companies shortlist you. That is your 'given' in this equation; you can't change it so don't sweat about it. The variables in your control are the tests conducted by the companies, group discussions (GDs) and interviews. Let's first go over the purpose of each. Written tests are conducted by companies to remove any false negatives, as opposed to false positives. That is, if your grades are good, your performance in the test will not matter too much; but if they are not good, the tests give you the chance to overwrite your academic record. Group discussions are conducted to eliminate the truly unsmart candidates. In a GD show maturity; try to demonstrate your thinking abilities and not your vocal strength or your English accent. Make sure you come forth as someone ahead of his years. As long as you stay calm, keep listening attentively and actively, you will definitely find an opportunity to speak (so don't get all nervous about it), and when your chance comes, make sure you make a point. Making a point is very different from uttering a sentence. It involves not just what you say but how you say it. Be calm, clear and coherent. Lastly, interviews are about revealing your personality. Don't try to be someone you are not. I have personally taken many campus interviews and students don't realize how transparent they are. The interviewer is able to judge very quickly from your demeanour and body language who you really are. Practising in front of the mirror is the best preparation for an interview. Make sure you stay relaxed all the time and come forth as a calm and confident person. That you are brainy and sharp is already established because you are in IIT, and you are already through with the GD and the test. So, even if you can't give correct answers to some questions in an interview, a smart interviewer will discount those as a one-off. However, if you show stress, lose your nerves, get rude or fumble in your speech, that is where the interview goes wrong.

The placement process will burn you out if you don't manage it well. It is assumed that in the four years on campus you have already matured into someone who can manage his time and energy well. If not, trouble will knock on your door. Carry snack bars in your bag because sudden changes in schedules occur and you could be stuck waiting for an interview for a couple of hours, or given a sudden repeat round of GD. In such cases, if your energy levels drop, your performance will be below par and your batchmates will grab the opportunity.

Above all, be a part of the solution rather than the problem. There are students and faculty working hard trying to get jobs for all the students. Respect their efforts and try to contribute as much as you can. If you can't do anything, at least recognize their efforts when you meet them, thank them and maybe treat them to a drink in the canteen. The best thing to do obviously is to be part of the placement committee. The advantage is that you will understand the process better and also get to interface directly with the representatives of the company. But be completely clear it gives you no advantage in actually getting placed. If anything, you risk early exposure and overexposure that may harm your chances. Once again, I speak from experience.

On the other hand, do not make placements out to be more important than they are. I have seen students fight with their friends, lose all hope, go into a shell or some other self-destruct mode when they fail to be placed as they had wished. Remember, it's just a job. Your friends who get some of the most coveted jobs on campus will leave them within eighteen months of joining. In fact, most first jobs last only a short while. Most people go with the popular opinion and take up whatever job people around them vouch for. You should not get into that mad race; talk to your alumni, use the relationships you have forged over the four years to get clarity on what a particular job entails and whether it suits your expectations. Always keep in mind that a job is a job is a job. So, don't overstress yourself. Feel free to explore opportunities where you will be eager to get up every morning and make some kind of an impact. Consider a few start-ups (thankfully, the scene in India has improved considerably) or maybe even carve a career in a rock band or as an author.

In Summary

Proactive thinking is very important. I do not advocate planning and scheming your way through IIT. Going with the flow and taking a few risks is what youth is all about. Yet your thoughts should have a structure of some kind. What I have said above is just an outline and of course only my opinion. Have I acted on it? Not in the least. If anyone had an unplanned and chaotic four years at IIT, it was me.* But then, I had never read a book like this. You can avoid disaster if you think proactively and not let circumstances dictate terms to you.

LIFE AFTER IIT?

Once you pass out of IIT and get into the so-called real world, you will find some big changes. You will find that your respect for IIT will actually grow with every passing day. There was the

* Vivek.

mess food that you hated—your company's food court will have worse food on certain days. There were the professors whom you found rude and indifferent—your bosses will be a hundred times worse. There were the peers who annoyed you—there will be colleagues who will annoy you much more. Above all, you will sense the special lens through which the world sees you—at times it takes the form of respect, at times of awe, at times of curiosity; but most of the time it is of jealousy. It grows on you, makes you feel special and makes you feel special for the brand that has been stamped on to you for the rest of your life. Before you know it, you feel guilty and grateful at the same time whenever you think of that place called IIT.

However, there is a flip side to the story. More than 30 lakh students graduate from various colleges in India every year. Only 10,000 of them are IITians. That leaves 29,90,000 non-IITians. So, those 4,90,000 competitors you left behind four years back are suddenly visible everywhere once you pass out of IIT. They are joined by another 25 lakh who were not even interested in engineering back then. There is, of course, prestige in having become an engineer from an IIT, but what about the non-engineer non-IITians? There are many extremely talented people in that group as well. This heterogeneity of talent is probably the rudest shock to most IITians who've been living a cocooned existence until now. It is time to wake up.

In the real world, your IIT brand gives you an advantage but not a walkover. In fact, it burdens you with the additional weight of expectations. You will find hard questions being asked about your career choices. I have personally encountered the following question ad nauseam—'If you are from IIT, what are you doing at such-and-such place?' Being from IIT means there is always something special you are supposed to do, somewhere special you are supposed to be. People use this to isolate you in the real world. The first thing you should do after graduating is to place your identity as an IITian as a secondary, preferably a tertiary part of yourself. It should come in the third or even fourth sentence of your introduction, not the first. What then should be your first two lines of introduction? Your primary identity is your work and your personality. You should excel in both. You will find new benchmarks in both domains—extremely competent professionals and inspiring human beings who are not IITians. Learn from them. Identify gaps in yourself and start filling them up right away. Try to feel like a normal human being.

What you should retain from IIT is your relationships, with the institute and its people. Don't let go your friends, your peers, your seniors, your professors. Keep them close. Continue to engage with the IIT fraternity through alumni events, informal gatherings and of course emails and social media. Start thinking very actively about ways of giving back to the system that has given so much to you. Believe me, there is so much you will get in life just because you are from the IIT system that it will be a perpetual load on your conscience if you don't repay the system and express your gratitude in material ways. Monetary paybacks are the easiest to do. Pitching in as a contributing member in events and committees is a very healthy practice. Keep visiting the campus occasionally. It might just keep the IITian alive inside you.

My IIT: Vivek

Every IITian has his own IIT—his own perception and his own special journey through IIT. I am no different. Mine has been a sinusoidal journey of ups and downs, of hope and despair, of bonding and break-ups, of being at the top of the class and at the bottom of the class. I have given you so much gyan on how to prepare for IIT; it would be unfair of me to not share what my preparation was like. I am from a small town, so there were no big corporate coaching houses in my town. In fact, back then this industry was not corporatized. Kota was famous more for wheat and rice than anything else. And I am reticent so I had just two awesome and very sensible friends at that time.

It started with the preparations for the National Talent Search Exam (NTSE). For this exam I had to study a lot of things that actually set the background for IIT studies. I joined the coaching that my friends suggested to me. I did group studies with them which involved a lot of discussions, joint problem-solving and of course general gossip. I led a very private life for two years with not too many outdoor activities. My entertainment was limited to music. My family was extremely supportive and let me use my time the way I wanted to. They had zero expectations from me, or never expressed them if they had any. All the pressure on me was what I created for myself. On an average I would be studying for two sessions of three to four hours every day—one of them with my study buddies and the other all by myself.

By the way, in case it helps you even one bit, here is a sample day in my life when I was preparing:

6 a.m.   Up from bed and into my private room, beginning to read something interesting, mostly physics. Maybe some problem-solving as well.

8 a.m.   Fresh from the morning read, time for some exercise. Put on some good music and pick up the dumbbells or just hard-core dancing for the next hour.

9 a.m.   Time for breakfast. A bell rings in my room when breakfast is ready downstairs.

11 a.m.   Fresh and ready, I now head to a friend's house for the afternoon.

Noon   Reach friend's house and spend the day solving problems together; topics of philosophy, history and girls being relieving interjections in between.

3 p.m.   Lunch with friend at his place, followed by a cycle ride back home.

6 p.m. After a quick rest/break at home, usually more music or generally strolling on the terrace, head out for coaching classes.

9 p.m. Back home for dinner, a short break for a quick chit-chat with family and back to the study room by 10.

10 p.m. Night-study time. NEVER pick anything fresh to study. Only revise what has already been covered during the day or solve problems from topics I am familiar with.

XX a.m. Turn in when feeling sleepy. There is no fixed 'sleeping time'. Only the waking hour is fixed!

Of course this comes with the following BIG disclaimers:

1. This was over a decade ago. The times were different. Television was not so interesting and there was no Internet.

2. This was in a small town where distances were small and there was more spare time in general.

3. This timetable applied exclusively to me, with my particular energy levels and sleeping and nutrition requirements.

4. This was me when I was fifteen years younger, so I can't work half as hard today if you ask me!

I don't remember taking many days off from this schedule. The intensity of study would increase at times, but not go down. Bunking school was common and affordable because the ICSE (Indian Certificate of Secondary Examination) syllabus was refreshingly easy to cope with. I probably bunked more than 30–40 per cent of my classes in school. I am an immensely competitive person, so I just wanted to beat everyone else, more than anything. JEE was a personal challenge for me but honestly I didn't know what I wanted to be or do in life.

Oh, and yes, I must mention here that I used to be a bit superstitious as well during my exam prep days. Things like touching the floor with the right foot first when stepping out of bed, making a wish under a bridge when a train was passing over it, sneezing an even number of times or starting to bathe with five mugs of water poured first before applying soap—these were some of the numerous good omens that I firmly believed in back then. I still remember the squirrel I saw on the tree outside during my JEE Physics paper. In fact, I was so superstitious that I considered it might actually have contributed to my success!

Unfortunately for me, all this remained exactly the same in my IIT days as well. It cost me the two major driving forces behind my achievements—sensible friends and a clear target. I found that I had a latent talent for dancing and did a lot of that in festivals and events. I also tried to forge one too many 'deep' relationships. The overinvestment in extracurricular activities and relationships hurt my academics. Thankfully, though, I settled down within a couple of years of my passing out of IIT and now have a fairly acceptable career.

When I look back on my IIT days I miss the friends and the dancing. I don't remember any classes or professors; whatever

I remembered has faded away in a decade. This is something I would advise you against. The IITs are the pinnacle of the Indian academic system. Every moment spent there is worth its weight in gold and you need to take the maximum advantage of it. Don't miss the academic part. Remember, that for each one of you inside, there are fifty outside the gates who would give an arm and a leg to get into IIT. Don't insult them by wasting your time there. The value of your chance makes selection into IIT, and clearing JEE itself, such a coveted and discussed thing in India and the world. So much so that it has spawned droves of authors, some from IIT itself—and one of them will now sign off and bid you all the best for this golden quest!

My IIT: Paras

IIT for me was a name unheard of till class ten. Coming from a small town and a family of doctors meant I had no knowledge of engineering and the various colleges and entrance exams around it. By a stroke of luck my father's friend happened to visit us after my class ten boards and asked me about my career plans. Naive as I was, I told him I wanted to do engineering. When he asked me about my college of choice I said MNIT (Motilal Nehru National Institute of Technology Allahabad), which was then MLNREC (Motilal Nehru National Regional Engineering College), as one of my cousins had gone there and that was the only college I knew. My father's friend was surprised and asked me if I had heard of IIT and Kota. An uncle's son was studying in Kota and that is how I found out about the IITs and JEE preparation. What ensued was an overnight journey to Kota, an entrance examination and two years of coaching in Kota. I didn't have a book like this to help me get through the paces of JEE preparation, so this is what I did.

I had virtually cracked JEE in class eleven itself. I worked hard and stayed disciplined about my studies. Though I did not have a particular schedule, my approach was to just get up and study if I felt like studying, no matter what time it was. This was something that I had to correct when I got closer to the JEE exam date since it's always better to stick to a schedule. I never missed a class in the entire two years and I made sure I was always moving in tandem with the class. Competing with very sharp students made me humble and helped me realize that JEE was not going to be a cakewalk. I had the privilege of being friends with some really smart peers and seniors who helped me every step of the way. I lost my path a little in class twelve and started wasting a lot of time watching movies, and so on. While it is easy to lose focus because of the long journey, make sure that you keep reminding yourself of the goal and don't get complacent at any stage.

Below is a rough schedule that I followed for two years:

Division of Hours

ACTIVITIES	CLASS XI		CLASS XII	
	Weekdays	Weekends	Weekdays	Weekends
Class Revision	2	NA	2	NA
Classroom Homework	2	NA	2	NA
Physics Practice (10 problems)	1	1	1	1
Chemistry Practice (10 problems)	1	1	1	1
Maths Practice (10 problems)	1	1	1	1
Revision of Old Topics	NA	6	NA	3
Revision of Class XI Topics	NA	NA	1	3
Sleep	7	8	7	8
School/Breaks/Sports	10	7	9	7

Finally, I did make it through JEE and went on to experience the phenomenon that is IIT. Like everyone else, I had my own experience, my own version of IIT. I had a lot of fun, did some studying, made some wonderful friends, rubbed a few people the wrong way, tried my hand at a lot of things and tried to soak in as much as I could. I never really cared about the grades and wasn't disciplined in the first year, so grades never really cared about me either (not for the first few terms at least!). I started a radio show on campus, edited the newsletter, went on a lot of trips, bunked a fair share of classes and labs, went on an exchange programme and cared for nothing and everything at the same time.

It is needless to say that I made my share of mistakes while at IIT but that is what youth is all about. One thing that I still regret is not making full use of the resources at IIT. I could have made more friends and learnt so much about life from them. Perhaps the biggest regret is that I didn't go to my professors for advice and didn't keep in touch with them after I left. Frankly, I think I made use of only a fraction of what IIT offered me.

People have often asked me what makes IIT special: is it the curriculum, the method of teaching or something else. My belief is that it's the confidence it gives you. When you walk out of the gates of IIT, you walk out as a confident person who is not afraid to take on any challenge. Four years with some of the brightest minds, the last-minute hustle to get concepts into your head and the endless *bakar* sessions leave you equipped with all the tools that you need to take on any challenge that life throws at you. This self-belief is what makes all the difference.

As to where I am after IIT, well, I left my first job within the first year and went on to start a chain of tea cafes in Delhi. I lost my mind and did an MBA, got into a job again. I am still trying to work out what I don't want in my life. The list is growing so hopefully I will figure out what I really want sometime soon.

The Private Glossary of an IITian

There is a feeling of guilt as we let this out of the bag. This is supposed to be stuff only a true IITian, who has been through the rites of passage, knows about. However, we feel that while we are sharing everything else it seems unfair to hold these back. Of course, these are just words. The true meaning of these will be known only once you are inside the gates.

SOBRIQUETS

The most important part of the IIT lingo is the sobriquets used to address people and certain things. Most of them are permanent based on either behavioural patterns or the courses one is taking or even the part of the country one comes from. All of these are used in good faith and there are no derogatory intentions in using them. Still, if publishing them here hurts a few sentiments we apologize for that upfront.

1. **Arbit**: One of the most frequently used words on campus, it refers to anyone or anything that does not make sense

(at least the level of sense one expects within an IIT campus). It is the shortened form of 'arbitrary'. For example, when everyone is discussing an engrossing topic, someone mentions something completely out of context and irrelevant. Or, someone is found roaming around the campus aimlessly. Done once or twice, just the mentioned thing or activity is arbit. Done more frequently, the person doing it is permanently labelled arbit.

2. **Arbit Kholu**: 'Kholu' is someone who keeps 'opening up' eccentric ideas all the time. Once the sobriquet of arbit becomes permanent for a person, the additional salutation of being an arbit kholu is at times used to qualify him.

3. **Baap/Maa**: For freshers, a senior student, usually from the third year, is appointed mentor for her/his initial days on campus. This person is supposed to protect and guide the new student. Usually the baap/maa cannot rag the fresher and ends up defending her/him if the latter is ragged beyond reasonable limits.

4. **Bachche/Fuchche**: Freshers on campus.

5. **Bajar**: Tough or hard. This can be applied to either subjects or questions in an exam. At times it is also used to describe strength in any domain. For example, someone could be a bajar gymnast. Note that this is applicable only to the efforts and not necessarily to the results. Bajar subjects are difficult

and take a toll on your time; they don't necessarily enlighten you.

6. **Bhokal**: Used for someone or something that is over the top and awesome. It also has to be something that is huge and immense in scale.

7. **Chaapu**: Someone who gets great results with sharpness and intelligence rather than through too much work. This sobriquet can also be extended to a thing or situation that demonstrates the 'work smart and achieve results' ethos.

8. **Chaatu**: This means very boring. It is typically applied to someone who is verbose, who talks a lot without saying anything and is particularly annoying to listen to. Like all our other sobriquets, this can be extended to situations and things, like books or classes.

9. **Chhaggi**: Someone who gets in the whereabouts of a 6 point GPA. This is also interchangeably used for a CGPA of 6. A word about grade points here: grade points in IIT are known by many different short forms like CPI, CGPA, GPA, etc. No one quite understands how or why these students end up getting the grades that they do. Life is easiest for those who get either As or Fs. For everyone in between, it is a confused continuum of uncertainty, and they usually gleefully accept any outcome that is 'at least better than an F'.

10. **Dassoo**: This belongs to the same family of sobriquets as chhaggi, and refers to someone who has a CGPA of 10 ('das' in Hindi). As you can guess, the epitome

of academic achievement in an IIT is someone who is a dassoo. Dassoos are born, they cannot be made. A unique concoction of being a chaapu, maggoo, lassoo and fundoo makes one a dassoo.

11. **Dep Kholu**: Dep stands for department and kholu stands for someone who opens something. A dep kholu is the student who 'opens up' a department in a specific IIT in a specific year, that is, he is the first entrant to that department by having the highest rank in that subject. So, if in IIT Kanpur in the year 2002 there were (hypothetically) five students in the chemistry department, the one with the highest hawa, or JEE rank, among them becomes the dep kholu of Chem of the '02 batch.

12. **Despo**: Not tough to understand this one; despo is short for desperate. A despo is someone who falls to undignified and uncool levels in the pursuit of a very specific desire. One can become a despo for a girl, another can become a despo in his attempts to get an A in a certain course. Despos annoy everyone around them by their fixation on their goal and the compromises on sobriety that they make in its pursuit.

13. **Dhakkan**: Polar opposite of the dep kholu, a dhakkan is the guy who has the last rank in any particular group of students, grouped either by batch or by department.

14 **Enthu**: An enthu is a valued customer. Enthu is short for enthusiasm and this trait is phenomenally valuable

on an IIT campus. With academic and peer pressure straining the nerves, someone with enthusiasm is always a welcome addition to any situation. An enthu is generally a person who exudes positivity and energy in most situations. He is valued in group assignments. He is valued in cultural events. He is valued in late-night bullas and tullas. An alternative usage of enthu is to denote enthusiasm itself.

15. **Fattu**: Fattu is someone who is chicken. He takes such little risk that his existence becomes utterly pointless at times and in fact becomes a liability in any major initiative. Fattus spend months doting on a girl but never look her in the eye; fattus never participate in aggressive shows of strength between hostels; fattus never venture out of campus late at night.

16. **Fodu**: Fodu is a person who achieves results in the toughest of situations, with remarkable consistency and predictability. Calling someone a fodu is safe since it does not presume any remark upon the means used to achieve the results. So a fodu could be a maggoo or a chaapu, he could be a lassoo or a dassoo, but he has achieved results and so he is a fodu. Fodu is generally used in narrower contexts, say specific to playing phatta, or cracking a quiz.

17. **Fraud**: A fraud is someone who is not serious. Someone who gets by without putting in the requisite effort. A fraud student is someone who bunks classes, does topa in assignments and exams, and fools people most of

the time. Even professors and courses are sometimes referred to as fraud if they just fill up the hours without actually achieving anything.

18. **Frustoo**: Frustoo is someone who has latent frustrations that manifest in obsessive-compulsive or unusually intense behaviour. For example, someone who resorts to negative behaviour like seclusion, drinking or arguing because he is performing poorly in academics and can't find a way to correct it is assumed to be academically frustrated. Someone who collects porn magazines and watches porn on his laptop a lot is assumed to be sexually frustrated and, once discovered, is labelled a frustoo. Frustoos are avoided for their explosive tendencies and negative influence.

19. **Fundoo**: Fundoo is someone who has unique and unconventional talents. For example, someone who is a great artist but has never competed or achieved mainstream success would be called a fundoo for his skills; but, because of his lack of achievements he cannot technically be called a chaapu. Someone who has a great grasp over quantum mechanics will be a fundoo, but if he doesn't score awesome grades to show it he cannot graduate into a fodu or a chaapu.

20. **Ghissu**: Ghissu is derived from ghisna, which can be roughly translated as scrubbing. A ghissu wastes inordinate amounts of time studying through inefficient and painstaking repetition. Ghissus making it into IIT

should be seen as a partial failure of the JEE system itself, because a ghissu would have cleared the examination by similar means, and it is very difficult to crack the JEE by rote and repetition.

21. **Hapa-hap/Hapax**: Hapa-hap is derived from the sound made when something is being done rapidly. Imagine someone eating in big mouthfuls and really fast. His hands and mouth go *hapa-hap, hapa-hap, hapa-hap*. So, anything that is bizarrely fast-paced is referred to as hapa-hap. People eat hapa-hap, they solve assignments hapa-hap. Hapax is just a shortened form of hapa-hap. At times, this can also be applied to size instead of speed or even be used as a general exclamation. For example, if someone looks unusually good one day, people would say she is looking hapax.

22. **Kantaap**: Most of the time this is used for a very attractive female student. The connotations are more towards sexy than beautiful. The word is derogatory and is used cautiously and privately.

23. **Kholu**: A kholu is someone who throws in a lot of street-smart concepts or comments during a regular conversation. These are actually logical traps for the uninitiated. Kholus are people who exhibit interesting patterns or give commentary which often astonishes a lay person.

24. **Lassoo**: This is someone adept at sycophancy. A lassoo could be doing lassa with professors or students of the

opposite sex to become their favourites and gain unfair advantage over others, maybe more competent students.

25. **Maggoo**: A maggoo learns by rote and hence spends a significant part of his time with books. He is probably slow to grasp concepts or insecure about his academic performance. He will voluntarily sacrifice precious leisure time on campus for academics.

26. **Senti**: Short for sentimental, this refers to an emotional person or someone very often in an emotionally charged state. Even actions can be classified as senti. Emotions can be of all kinds, from doting on the opposite sex, being overly possessive about something or someone, to displaying undue anger or perturbation.

27. **Stud/Bond/God**: A student who is supremely good-looking and is perceived to be significantly above the rest in terms of talent and potential. The perception need not be substantiated through actual events.

ACTIVITIES

Things that one does on the campus fall into repeatable patterns. Patterns that are repeated most often acquire specific names. Some of the most popular activities on campus are given below.

1. **Apping**: The process of writing and submitting applications to colleges for higher studies, typically for an MS degree in the US or other developed countries.

This is a hectic activity for second- and third-year students as they fervently vie to get some exposure in other great colleges after IIT. Reaching out to professors, filling online forms, sending international packages by airmail and getting money transferred in euros and dollars is all part of apping.

2. **Bakar**: Bakar is the act of chattering away in groups on specific topics. This can get very intense. For example, students can have heated discussions on whether dogs make better pets or cats. The trivial nature of the topic and its irrelevance to things that matter in real life on an IIT campus qualify a discussion as a bakar.

3. **Bhasad**: Bhasad refers loosely to pandemonium. It is used when a high volume of mostly confusing activity is unleashed just to attract attention and create the feeling of a lot happening. For example, one can fill in reams of writing sheets when answering a question and create bhasad without actually solving the problem. Or one can have a lot of meetings and post a lot of notices/posters for an event, creating a chaotic buzz and causing confusion and consternation all around.

4. **Bulla**: This is a more relaxed form of chit-chat, as opposed to bakar. Here the topic of conversation is virtually non-existent and the conversation meanders aimlessly across various threads. It is a very relaxing form of passing time and happens only among people who generally enjoy talking to each other. Mostly, people share memories or

talk about personal stuff when doing bulla. Bakar, on the other hand, is impersonal and seemingly far more topical and intense than bulla.

5. **Chaapna/Taapna**: The innocent crime of copying from someone else's work in exams or assignments. It is accepted among the student community but frowned upon and severely reprimanded by the professors.

6. **Fight**: Fight, or fight maarna, is the act of putting in a lot of sincere effort to recover from academic lows. People put in fight to become dassoos.

7. **Intro**: The act of introducing oneself, mostly to seniors during ragging.

8. **Kela**: A setback due to an unfortunate turn of events, rather than any shortage of ability or effort, usually referred to in a light-hearted manner. For example, if someone didn't get the room he wanted in the hostel due to preferential allotment to someone else, it can be said that '*Uska kela ho gaya*'.

9. **Machana/Phodna/Crack Machana**: Doing amazing things and achieving astonishingly great results.

10. **Night Out**: A night spent waking, and doing either studies or bulla or tulla. A very common pastime as time is always short on campus.

11. **Phatta**: Playing cricket with idiosyncratic rules like one-tip-one-hand out, hitting outside a certain line directly means out, hitting a tree means 5 runs, etc.

12. **Poltu**: Political activities related to elections, etc.

13. **Proxy**: Standing in or filling in for someone else. Mostly used in the context of attendance where a student speaks or signs on behalf of someone missing from the class to mark his attendance illegally on the records. Severely frowned upon by the authorities and carries disciplinary repercussions if discovered.

14. **Sentiyapa**: An extension of 'senti', this is an activity that is emotionally loaded, like an emotional conversation.

15. **Topa**: The act of copying someone else's work.

16. **Tulla**: Generally roaming around with friends to kill time, chit-chatting and loafing.

SHORT FORMS

The last set of terms comprises campus short forms, acronyms and nicknames used for places or things that are found within the walls of an IIT. Some of the best-known ones are below.

1. **Acad**: Academics. Also used for the entire academic area that houses lecture theatres, library, computer centre, etc.

2. **Admin**: Administrative area and staff. This is the set of people and offices where all administrative work happens, like fee payments, course registrations, form submissions, etc.

3. **CC**: Computer Centre, a place where the institute's community can access the central computing resources. With increased access to laptops and smartphones, and

with most services available on the cloud, physical visits to the CC in the IITs are reducing.

4. **Convo**: Convocation, the day and ceremony when the passing-out batch officially receives the degrees.

5. **DR1**: The student with the highest CGPA in any department in a given batch in an IIT.

6. **Diro**: The institute Director.

7. **DOSA**: Dean of Student Affairs.

8. **Farra**: Quick tips, summary or formulae written on a piece of paper used as a quick reference when delivering a lecture. Also used as a cheat sheet in exams for copying from.

9. **Fuddu/Fuddi**: A PhD student in IIT—male or female.

10. **Fukka**: An F grade.

11. **Gult**: Someone from the southern states of India.

12. **Gymkhana**: The official representative body of students.

13. **Hawa/AIR**: All India Rank, whose acronym is AIR, which translates into hawa in Hindi.

14. **HOD**: Head of Department.

15. **Ikka/Bikka/Sikka/Dikka**: Nicknames for grades A, B, C and D.

16. **IR1**: The fresher with the highest hawa, or JEE rank, among all the students of a certain batch in a specific IIT.

17. **Junta**: The general body of students.

18. **Load**: Tension or pressure.

19. **LT**: The lecture theatres where classes are held.

20. **Matka/Matki**: Nickname for male and female MTech students.

21. **PPO**: Pre-placement offer. This is made by some companies to students who have interned with them before the official placements began.

22. **PPT**: Pre-placement talk. A talk or presentation that most companies planning to visit campus for hiring give to the students. It is considered important to keep the halls full during a PPT from a company that offers good jobs, so that the top bosses of that company carry away a good impression of the batch with them. Students interested in a job with that company attend these sessions and look to doing lassa with the bosses of the company before or after the PPT.

23. **SAC(k)**: Student Activity Centre, the nerve centre of all official extracurricular activities on campus.

24. **TA**: A teaching assistant in the labs or in the class.

25. **Tute**: Tutorials, where follow-up work is done on lectures. Assignments are solved, problems are discussed and supplemental course material is shared.

25. **Zuk/Zukki**: A zero scored in an exam or assignment. Believe it or not, it is a very common score in courses at IIT. The most brilliant students from the country, after passing the all-important JEE are seriously humbled when they are given zeroes in their exams by the faculty.